PENGUIN
SPECIALS

Penguin Specials fill a gap. Written by some of today's most exciting and insightful writers, they are short enough to be read in a single sitting – when you're stuck on a train; in your lunch hour; between dinner and bedtime. Specials can provide a thought-provoking opinion, a primer to bring you up to date, or a striking piece of fiction. They are concise, original and affordable.

To browse digital and print Penguin Specials titles, please refer to **penguin.com.au/penguinspecials**

OTHER TITLES BY SEAN DORNEY

Papua New Guinea: People, Politics and History since 1975

The Sandline Affair: Politics and Mercenaries and the Bougainville Crisis

LOWY INSTITUTE
FOR INTERNATIONAL POLICY

The Lowy Institute is an independent, nonpartisan international policy think tank. The Institute provides high-quality research and distinctive perspectives on the issues and trends shaping Australia's role in the world. The Lowy Institute Papers are peer-reviewed essays and research papers on key international issues affecting Australia and the world.

For a discussion on *The Embarrassed Colonialist* with Sean Dorney and some of Australia's most prominent political commentators, visit the Lowy Institute's daily commentary and analysis site, *The Interpreter*: **lowyinterpreter.org/ EmbarrassedColonialist**.

Sean Dorney is a Nonresident Fellow at the Lowy Institute. After reporting on the Pacific (with a particular focus on Papua New Guinea) for over four decades, Sean left the ABC in August 2014. During his time with the ABC he won a Walkley for his coverage of the Aitape tsunami and was both deported and awarded an MBE by the Papua New Guinean Government. He is the author of *Papua New Guinea: People, Politics and History since 1975* and *The Sandline Affair: Politics and Mercenaries and the Bougainville Crisis.*

LOWY INSTITUTE
FOR INTERNATIONAL POLICY

The Embarrassed Colonialist

A LOWY INSTITUTE PAPER

SEAN DORNEY

PENGUIN BOOKS

UK | USA | Canada | Ireland | Australia
India | New Zealand | South Africa | China

Penguin Books is part of the Penguin Random House group of companies
whose addresses can be found at global.penguinrandomhouse.com.

Penguin
Random House
Australia

First edition published by Penguin Group (Australia), 2016

Printed and bound in Australia by Griffin Press,
an accredited ISO AS/NZS 14001 Environmental Management Systems printer.

ISBN: 9780143573951

penguin.com.au

CONTENTS

Introduction.. I

A personal journey.. 5

Some history 11

PNG's challenges 27

PNG's strengths.. 49

Why Australia needs to re-engage...................... 72

What should be done? 93

Forty years on... 113

Endnotes 121

Acknowledgements 135

Introduction

Lawrence Stephens, chairman of Papua New Guinea's high-profile anti-corruption non-government organisation, Transparency International PNG, tells of boarding a flight to PNG from Cairns.

'I walked up to the woman with the Geiger counter who was going to check if I was a terrorist with a bomb. And brushing me down she said, "Oh, are you catching the flight to Nagoya?" I said, "No, I'm catching the flight to Papua New Guinea." She looked shocked, and asked why I was going there. When I explained it is my home, she said she could think of nowhere worse! I told her I could think of half a dozen places that would be worse, and asked if she had ever been to PNG? "No," she said. "And I have no intention of going there!"'[1]

Stephens' encounter with an Australian official

might be an extreme example of the ignorance and disdain with which Australians seem to view PNG these days, but it is by no means an isolated one. 'You jump in a cab down in Australia, whether it be Sydney or Brisbane,' says Kostas Constantinou, chairman of PNG's largest bank, Bank South Pacific, and owner of several hotels in Port Moresby, 'and you get an Aussie taxi driver and he says, "Where are you going, mate?" "I'm going up to Papua New Guinea." And they say, "What! Are you insane? What are you going to that place for?"'[2]

This is not to say that PNG's – or more particularly Port Moresby's – reputation for lawlessness and violence is not well deserved. Constantinou's father, Sir George Constantinou, established the extremely successful construction company Hebou Constructions (PNG). He was murdered in Port Moresby in 2008 when he was carjacked while visiting one of the company's timber mills. When I was the ABC correspondent based in Port Moresby, I was mugged twice. Once when some *raskols* (the generic name for young criminals in PNG) held a screwdriver to my throat and stole my wallet, and a second time when they put a gun to my temple, punched me to the ground and stole the ABC vehicle.

The fact that violence and lawlessness in Port Moresby have come to colour our view of PNG as a whole speaks to a deeper ambivalence about our nearest neighbour and perhaps even embarrassment about our role as its former colonial master. On 16 September 2015, PNG celebrated its fortieth anniversary of independence, yet the milestone barely rated a mention in Australia. At around half a billion dollars a year, Australia gives more aid to PNG than to any other country – yet Australians seem to know little and care less about the country. The 2015 Lowy Institute Poll revealed, for example, that 61 per cent of Australians could not identify Peter O'Neill, PNG's prime minister.[3] How many Australians realise that PNG was once an Australian colony?

The aim of this Paper is to help change this situation. The first half of the Paper will look at PNG today, reflecting on both its problems, which are written and talked about often, but also its strengths, which rarely rate a mention. This first part of the Paper will also examine how Australia has contributed to both the country's weaknesses and strengths, first as the colonial power and, since independence, as PNG's main donor. In doing this, my aim is not just to educate Australians a little about PNG, but also to inspire them to be more interested in it. So in the second half of this Paper I will explore why we cannot continue to ignore PNG, and will conclude with some ideas about how we can strengthen our relationship.

Forty years after PNG's independence, Australia needs to accept, rather than escape, its colonial past. It needs to do so not in any negative or paternalistic sense; I am certainly not suggesting that the best way to deal with PNG's many problems is for Australia to resume a colonial posture. Rather, we need to acknowledge our colonial past as a starting point for a deeper engagement with PNG today. Australia's role in PNG, both in the past and present, needs to be taught in schools. There needs to be greater media attention paid to PNG. There should be more effort to build people-to-people connections with a particular focus on younger generations. And, once and for all, Australia needs to shed its embarrassment and embrace its relations with its nearest neighbour.

A personal
journey

PNG's post-colonial history has not just been a professional interest of mine. PNG gained its independence not long after I became a journalist. For forty years my career and personal life have been deeply entwined with the country.

In early 1974, I was a young journalist not long out of my three-year cadetship at the ABC when I was asked if I would go to Papua New Guinea to work on secondment with the then newly created National Broadcasting Commission (NBC). I had recently fallen out with the ABC's Queensland news editor, who had written me a letter saying that if I thought further fields were greener he would do nothing to stand in my way. I jumped at the 'greener fields' offer – probably the smartest thing I ever did.

The NBC came into being following PNG's

self-government at the end of 1973 through the combination of what had been the ABC network in our colony (radio stations in Port Moresby, Lae and Rabaul broadcasting in English) and the Australian administration's provincial radio service (radio stations in the provinces broadcasting in Melanesian pidgin, Hiri Motu and local languages). Some ABC journalists remained in PNG working for the NBC but quite a few had left and the NBC's first news editor, Albert Asbury, was looking for some young ABC journalists to fill the gaps. One of the facilities the ABC had handed over to the NBC was the Wonga Hostel, where I was allocated a room in the male accommodation wing.

I arrived in PNG wide-eyed and determined to be non-judgemental. In my rush to pack I had forgotten to bring a toothbrush so I ventured down the road from the hostel and found a trade store where all I could locate was a nail brush with a handle. 'These Papua New Guineans may have big teeth,' I thought. So I bought it. And for a day or two I stretched my lips apart as I brushed until I found a supermarket that, much to my relief, sold regular toothbrushes.

It was a great time to be a young journalist in PNG and I was afforded opportunities that would never have been possible in Queensland. Papua New Guinea was on its way to full independence and I was put on the parliamentary round. I covered all of the debates as PNG developed its Constitution. When Fiji's then prime minister, Ratu Sir Kamisese Mara, came to PNG to help Michael Somare convince people of the benefits of independence, I travelled around the country and was astounded by its diversity. Apart from the mainland – which PNG shares with Indonesia – there are 600 islands making up 15 per cent of PNG's landmass. Administratively PNG is divided into twenty-two provinces but there are four major regions: Papua, the Highlands, the northern coastal provinces and the New Guinea Islands (Manus, New Ireland, New Britain and Bougainville). While the vast majority of Papua New Guineans are Melanesian, the tiny populations of the Western Islands of the Manus Province are Micronesian and those in the atolls to the east of Bougainville are Polynesian.

Later, after independence in September 1975, I was one of three NBC journalists who provided a weekly wrap-up of the proceedings in parliament in PNG's three official languages. I reported in English while Arne Dougal, from the Simbu Province, broadcast his in Melanesian pidgin, and Tekura Age, from the Central Province, put out his weekly commentary in Hiri Motu.

One of my colleagues in the newsroom, John Harangu, from the East Sepik Province, invited me to join him in playing rugby league for Paga Panthers in the Port Moresby A-Grade competition. Through rugby league I met Papua New Guineans from a wide range of occupations and formed many solid friendships. I also had a bit of success on the field and ended up playing halfback for the national rugby league side, the Kumuls, in 1975 and captaining the team in my last outing the following year.

But 1975 was not only the year of PNG's independence. It was also the year I met my future wife. Pauline Nare was the first female broadcaster employed to work in the NBC's provincial radio station in her home province of Manus. They flew her down to Port Moresby to do a three-month broadcast training course at NBC headquarters and she was given a room in the female wing of the Wonga Hostel.

I found out some years later that she was not as impressed with me on first sight as I was with her. At a family function back in Australia, when I was asked how we first met, I explained I was sitting in the foyer of Wonga Hostel when I saw her come down the stairs for lunch. I was so struck by her looks that I was determined to get to know her. When asked by my brothers and sisters for the memory of her impression, Pauline replied, '"Oh," I thought, "that poor white guy. He's cross-eyed!"'

It got even worse when we went home to Pauline's village on Manus after we were married in 1976. Pauline's uncle, Wamok, who listened to the NBC radio commentary on rugby league, was apparently looking forward to meeting the Kumul captain who, he assumed, would be an impressive physical specimen. When we hopped off the boat onto the beach at the village, Uncle Wamok said something to Pauline in their native language. I asked her what he had said but she didn't tell me. Some years later, when she was cross with me for something, she said, 'You know what Uncle Wamok said that day? He said, "If you were a fish we would have thrown you back in!"'

The ABC pulled me back to Queensland at the end of my three-year secondment to the NBC but we returned to PNG in 1979 with our two young children when the ABC appointed me as its PNG correspondent. Five years later, in 1984, the PNG Government deported me after a major row with the ABC over a *Four Corners* program on the troubles that PNG was having that year in relation to its land border with Indonesia. I had put Alan Hogan from *Four Corners* in touch with contacts of mine on the border, which resulted in him getting an interview with one of the military commanders of the Free West Papua Movement, the OPM. The PNG Government was not happy.

By 1987 I had left the ABC and was working as a press secretary to the chief minister of the Northern Territory, when the ABC asked me whether I would go back to PNG as a correspondent. Once again I jumped at the chance and then spent another twelve years as the ABC's man in Port Moresby. In 1990, the then prime minister, Sir Rabbie Namaliu, who as foreign minister had ordered my deportation, awarded me an MBE.

That is PNG – endlessly bewildering. In this Paper, I hope to share some of the passion I have for this fascinating country that Australia once ruled.

Some history

Australia never spent a great deal of money on Port Moresby when it was the headquarters of Australia's colonial administration. Indeed, the contrast between what the British had built in Suva during their colonial governance of Fiji and what Australia constructed in Port Moresby for its administration of PNG is revealing. The stone and concrete Suva buildings are majestic examples of colonial architecture. In Konedobu, on the shores of the Port Moresby harbour, the Australian administration consisted of a collection of unimpressive wooden buildings, some quite ramshackle.

Australia, it seemed, was determined to pretend that it was not a colonial power. 'I wouldn't say that any Australians thought we had a colony,' Dame Rachel Cleland, the widow of Sir Donald Cleland, administrator from 1952 to 1967, told the ABC's *Taim Bilong Masta* social history radio series in the early 1980s. 'That was not in any way the thinking. The first time I heard "colony" mentioned was about 1965; and it gave me a distinct shock.'[4] Bertie Heath, a pioneer pilot in PNG, told the same program: 'We are not colonials. The Germans were colonials. The British were colonials . . . Am I going to be called a bloody colonial in this country?'[5]

Of course, the truth is that we were colonials – something that does not fit well with the view that Australians hold of ourselves. We are a nation that evolved from a convict settlement, name Ned Kelly as an iconic figure and our favourite national song is about somebody who stole sheep. So it is probably no surprise that we do not celebrate that as a nation we ruled over another people. The British readily acknowledge their imperial history and take pride in having had a British Empire that is now the British Commonwealth. Not us. It is because of our seeming reluctance to fully address our history in PNG and look rigorously at the consequences that I have coined the term 'embarrassed colonialist'.

GERMAN NEW GUINEA AND PAPUA
Queensland was still a colony of the British Empire when it tried to claim the eastern half of the island

of New Guinea in the early 1880s. The British repudiated the annexation. According to the late Professor Hank Nelson from the Australian National University, it was because the British 'were not willing to allow colonies to gather colonies'.[6] Nevertheless, with the Australian colonies badgering the British about German intentions and the threat their expanding activity might pose, Britain began negotiating with Germany about dividing eastern New Guinea in two. In November 1884, within days of each other, the Germans raised their flag at Rabaul on the island of New Britain in the New Guinea islands and the British the Union Jack in Port Moresby.

The Germans called their colony Kaiser-Wilhelmsland, and chartered a private business firm, *die Neuguinea-Kompagnie* (the New Guinea Company), to run it. The company pursued an aggressive policy of economic exploitation, which continued after direct German government control began in 1899. By the outbreak of the First World War, more than 280 000 hectares of land on the island of New Britain alone had been alienated and more than 100 000 islanders had been pressed into service as plantation labourers, one quarter dying on the job. Australia took effective control of British New Guinea after Federation and the name was changed to Papua under the Papua Act of 1905.[7]

Unlike the colonial process in some other parts of the world where the colonising power subdued, dominated, and then recruited indigenous political leaders, in PNG there was no unified system of pre-colonial administration. There were no large tribes or regional despots. The people were scattered into small and warring groups. Speaking about the work of the Australian Patrol Officers, who were known as *kiaps* (Melanesian pidgin from the German word for 'captain'), Professor Nelson said:

> A problem in Papua New Guinea is that the traditional political units were so small. There was no centralised system that the colonial power could take over and modify. It was a case of imposing Western law over an infinite variety of subtly changing local customs and values. The process had to be repeated over and over again. The Australian field . . . officers did not oversee the work of sultans or chiefs.[8]

In a land where 860 different indigenous languages exist, it was a system that demanded close, constant control if it was to be effective.

AUSTRALIA'S COLONIAL POSSESSION
When World War I began, the first significant Australian action was to seize German New Guinea.

The first Australian servicemen killed in the war, Captain Brian Pockley and Able Seaman William Williams, died in that action. After the war, at the Paris Peace Conference, Prime Minister Billy Hughes demanded that Australia be given permanent control of German New Guinea. Despite opposition from the prime minister of Great Britain and the president of the United States, he won for Australia a League of Nations mandate. That led to the establishment of separate Australian administrations. German New Guinea became the mandated territory of New Guinea and Papua remained a territory of Australia.

New Guinea and Papua were run quite differently. Very little land was taken from the people for tropical crops in Papua. Sir Hubert Murray, the first and longest-serving Lieutenant-Governor of Papua, argued that he should be given responsibility for New Guinea too. But the Australian Government decided that the land alienated from the indigenous people by the Germans would provide an excellent soldier settlement scheme. The plantations were expropriated, the Germans turned out of their homes and Australian ex-servicemen encouraged to take up a new life.

The Australian administration in New Guinea was under orders to try to make the mandated territory pay for itself. A gold rush at Bulolo in the late 1920s helped generate some revenue, but the administration's frugal spending on matters such as indigenous welfare and education also kept costs low.

Australia's annual report to the League of Nations' Permanent Mandates Commission in 1921 revealed that Australia spent £12 (A$24) on native education that year. Fifteen years later, in 1936, the Commission questioned whether the priority Australia put on 'native education' – at 1 per cent of the Territory's budget – was high enough.[9] By the outbreak of the Second World War in 1939, Australia had spent less on 'native' education in the 1930s than it had in the 1920s.

In Papua, Sir Hubert Murray was constantly starved of cash. He was also regularly under attack from resident Europeans for allegedly being 'absurdly paternal' by inhibiting their attempts to expand their commercial activities. Sir Hubert won a worldwide reputation for his benevolent governorship of Papua and his protection of the indigenous people. He was still in office when the Second World War began. Aged seventy-eight, he received instructions that in the event of an attack on Port Moresby he was to retire inland and direct guerrilla activities. His son, who had become a professional soldier, had already been retired by then on the grounds of age.

As many as half a million Australian military

personnel served in Papua New Guinea during the Second World War. My father, Kiernan 'Skipper' Dorney, was one of them. A doctor, he became Australia's most highly decorated medical officer in the war. In November 1943, he was a Major in charge of a section of the 2/3 Australian Field Ambulance. His unit was with the 2/32 Infantry Battalion, which had captured the strategically important Pabu Hill inland from Finschhafen on the northern coastline. The Japanese then cut them off and for five days they were subjected to heavy fire from Japanese artillery, mortars and small arms. The Japanese also attempted to infiltrate their position. Seventeen Australian soldiers were killed and fifty-seven were wounded. My father was awarded the Distinguished Service Order. His citation reads: 'Major Dorney, without sleep for five days, tended the wounded of his section, which was continually subjected to mortar fire. Many times he personally helped under fire to bring in the wounded.'[10]

POST-WAR ORDER

Like many Australians engaged in the campaign in New Guinea during the Second World War, my father came to have a high regard for the Papua New Guineans who helped our troops. That generation of Australians who fought in New Guinea is almost gone now. And so many other links have frayed. But back in July 1945, the Australian Government acknowledged that it owed 'a debt of gratitude' to the PNG people and it promised a new post-war order. A single administration – the Territory of Papua and New Guinea – was created. In the first five years after the war, the budget given to the unified administration by the Labor government totalled £16 million – forty times what had been spent on both territories in the five years leading up to the war.

Paul Hasluck became the Minister for Territories with responsibility for PNG in 1951, during the first Menzies government. He held the portfolio for twelve years and dominated the formulation of policy and even the details of administration. After his retirement, Sir Paul wrote in his book *A Time for Building* that he returned from his first trip to PNG in 1951:

> revolted at the imitation of British colonial modes and manners by some of the Australians who were there to serve the Australian Government . . . and never before in my life had I come across so many Australians who had lost so quickly any capacity to clean their own shoes or pour themselves a drink without the attention of a "boy".[11]

Hasluck was a demanding minister, never happy with the standard of performance of the Territory administration. Sir Paul was also critical of his fellow ministers in the Menzies government for not appreciating Australia's obligations as administrator. 'One disillusionment is that in my twelve years as Minister for Territories, Cabinet never had a thorough and well-informed discussion of our policy and objectives in Papua New Guinea although I was always trying to get one.'[12] In debates in Cabinet on the budget, he said there was no consideration as to goals.

> The most devastating objection to an increase [in funding] concerned the capacity of the Administration to use the money granted and the weakness of its financial control, but Cabinet never concerned itself with the attendant problem of Australian responsibility to make the Administration efficient. At times it almost seemed as though the view held was that, since Australia had met imperfectly its responsibility to govern the Territory efficiently and provide adequate staff, it had lessened its obligation to provide funds.[13]

The next Australian minister with responsibility for Papua New Guinea was Charles Edward ('Ceb')

Barnes of the Country Party, who held the job for eight years. He rejected Hasluck's suggestion as to who should head the Department of Territories and chose his own man from the Department of Trade. Neither believed PNG was anywhere near ready for independence and they were not about to hurry things along. In 1970 – just five years before PNG did get its independence – there were a total of 122 Papua New Guineans doing their sixth year of secondary schooling and only seven university graduates.

Grand Chief Sir Michael Somare recalls a confrontation with Barnes in 1968, the year Somare was first elected to the pre-independence House of Assembly. In an interview for this Paper, Sir Michael says he and others formed what he called 'a radical group' – the Pangu Pati. 'There is one incident I remember very well,' Sir Michael says. 'We were at ANGAU House, Australia New Guinea House, it's still standing today. And the Australian Minister for External Territories, Ceb Barnes, used to come up and talk to people and they decided that my group, which was calling for early self-government, should meet him. And Minister Barnes told us, "You people will never get your independence for Papua New Guinea!" And I was angry. And in an outburst I told him, "You give me the opportunity to educate my fellow Papua New Guineans and we will make our independence in ten years' time!". That was in 1968. And we did it in seven years. I shortened and beat my own prediction. And we got it in 1975.'[14]

INDEPENDENCE

Gough Whitlam travelled to Papua New Guinea as opposition leader in 1969 and made PNG an election issue in Australia – for perhaps the first and only time. He advocated that an early date be set for the end of Australian colonial rule. He proposed that self-government should be granted as early as 1972.

On two highly publicised follow-up trips in 1970 and 1971, Whitlam travelled to the Gazelle Peninsula in East New Britain where some of the Tolai people were agitating for greater control over their own affairs. There was also trouble brewing for the Australian administration on Bougainville over land matters relating to the opening of CRA's Bougainville Copper mine. Although Ceb Barnes acknowledged in April 1971 that self-government might follow PNG's next national election, he was removed as minister and a youthful Andrew Peacock brought a new approach to dealing with PNG. After the PNG election in 1972, which resulted in Somare patching together an unlikely coalition of parties and interest groups, Peacock struck up a very positive rapport with the mostly young, new political leaders in Port

Moresby. That general election was only the third ever held in PNG. Whitlam won power in Australia in December 1972, and Papua New Guinea became self-governing at the end of 1973 and independent in September 1975.

Australia could not have delayed giving PNG its independence for many more years without witnessing far more strife and consequently far greater post-independence problems. The debate is not 'Did PNG get independence too early?' but 'Did the preparations start too late?' Somare is fairly blunt about it: 'Australia did not put in enough effort to prepare us,' he says. 'Even a lot of people who became district commissioners, some of them have admitted, "Yes, it was a mistake we made. We never prepared. The Territory was never prepared for those changes."'[15] There was a lot to be done. The Highlands did not really get opened up until the 1950s and in 1970 there was still an area of some 170 000 hectares classified as not being under administrative control. There is no doubt that many of the Australian *kiaps*, school teachers, health workers, missionaries and others performed some extraordinarily heroic work in often very challenging circumstances.[16]

Will Muskens, who was a *kiap* from 1958 to 1975, says it has always struck him as a missed opportunity that Australia did not enter into a treaty with Papua

New Guinea so that more of those who had spent valuable years in PNG could have stayed on working alongside their Papua New Guinean counterparts. He believes that a treaty could have kept doctors, teachers, agricultural advisers, technical and trade specialists and *kiaps* in PNG for a few more years. 'Such an agreement could have been subject to terms that could be reviewed every twelve months, with salaries paid for by the Australian Government,' Muskens says. 'I envisaged a scheme that would transfer all of these Australian officers to a special unit in the Department of Foreign Affairs seconded to PNG, but under the direction and control of the relevant PNG departments.'[17] But in our haste to leave after independence, we offered all these people golden handshakes. 'While I, and a large number of my colleagues, opted to leave under the terms of the Employment Security Scheme,' Muskens continues, 'which literally encouraged us to take the money and run, I feel certain that if the Australian Government had been seriously committed to retaining our services I would have stayed on.'[18]

FORGOTTEN PNG

Inevitably, those thousands of Australians who did work in PNG prior to independence are fast thinning out. Fewer and fewer Australians have any real knowledge of this fascinating country to Australia's north, which we were responsible for bringing to nationhood. This lack of understanding affects our dealings. The Australian media generally ignores PNG. And too few of those advising on or deciding on policy seem to show any deep, abiding interest. As one senior figure in Canberra told me, in the corridors of Parliament House 'the lowliest adviser and the backest of back benchers can give you chapter and verse about the Middle East, but you could probably walk into a Cabinet meeting and talk about PNG and everyone will stare at you and blink'.

There are exceptions. Foreign Minister Julie Bishop has a fond attachment to Papua New Guinea. 'My Year Nine teacher at school thought, rather presciently,' she told a group of rising PNG and Australian leaders at the Lowy Institute in late 2013, 'that the fourteen year olds in her charge should learn a bit more about Australia's closest neighbours. And so it was that I, and the other girls in my class, became penpals in 1970 with a class of fourteen-year-old boys at the Martyrs School in Popondetta. Sadly, my correspondence with young Oscar of Oro Province petered out, but recently I spoke of my penpal and produced a faded photograph that he had sent to me.'[19] The *PNG Post-Courier* tried to track him down – but a few too many Oscars came forward claiming to be the lost penpal, some surprisingly young.

In the year of PNG's independence, Bishop's sister, Patricia, did her medical internship in Papua New Guinea working in Goroka. And in 2014, her niece, Isabel, also went to Goroka to work as a volunteer teacher at *Buk Bilong Pikinini* (Books for Children – Children's Library). Bishop's family connection goes even further. Her uncle, Ross, fought in PNG in the Second World War and her great uncle, Harry Penny, founded the Teachers' College in PNG in the 1960s. 'So Papua New Guinea has captured my imagination,' she said, 'as a place of extraordinary landscapes, rich history and, of course, the most warm-hearted people.'[20]

A politician from the other side, Shadow Minister for Immigration and Border Protection Richard Marles, also has a link to the Martyrs School. In 1984, Marles spent three days as a sixteen year old staying at Martyrs on a school trip. 'We climbed Mount Lamington, which was a volcano that erupted in the 1950s,' he tells me. 'We did that with our contemporaries from Martyrs, which was a great experience.' As a parliamentary secretary in the Rudd and Gillard governments, Marles travelled the world securing support for Australia's membership of the UN Security Council. But in his opinion nowhere else compares with PNG. 'We have on our doorstep the most exotic country in the world. Life is lived in Papua New Guinea in a way that it is lived nowhere else on the planet,' Marles says. 'It is genuinely remarkable and I think we Australians are incredibly lucky to have PNG as a neighbour. What an utterly amazing place! But I don't think that sort of amazement and that wonder about PNG is at all understood in Australia.' He says the level of ignorance is frustrating. 'We used to be the world experts on Papua New Guinea and now the level of study and literature in Australia has gone down dramatically.'[21]

We should turn that around.

PNG's challenges

If Papua New Guinea has any public image in Australia at all, it is that of a small, violent and underdeveloped country with a lot of big problems. While Australians do need to know more about PNG generally – its history, culture and politics – there is no point in glossing over the many challenges that PNG does face. In fact, there are important practical reasons why Australians need to be more conscious of PNG's problems. Australia still invests heavily in PNG's development and so understanding these problems more fully is key to working with PNG to address them.

Leaving aside PNG specialists, there is not a lot of discussion about what role Australia may have played in causing these problems in the first place, and what role we may now be playing in sustaining or exacerbating them. I'm not suggesting that problems like corruption and failures of law and order were or are all Australia's fault. PNG is a sovereign state and it is the responsibility of its leaders to address its national failings. But if we are going to work towards a better and more productive bilateral relationship we need to acknowledge and understand some of the sins of the past.

A lot has been written about PNG's shortcomings and development needs. It is not a short list. But in my experience four closely related areas stand out: PNG's imperfect democracy; poorly thought out and executed development policies; high levels of corruption; and lawlessness and lack of order.

IMPERFECT DEMOCRACY

Sir Paul Hasluck may have been frustrated at what he regarded as the limited success of what Australia achieved in PNG on his watch from 1951 to 1962, but there is no doubt that PNG was much easier to administer under autocratic colonial rule than it has been as an independent, democratic country. While PNG's population has tripled since 1975, the post-colonial collapse in the delivery of many services in rural Papua New Guinea is directly attributable to the way politics has infused almost every aspect of its administration. Under colonial rule, the Australian

Patrol Officers, the *kiaps*, had undoubted authority. 'God's Shadow on Earth' was the title of one of the *Taim Bilong Masta* radio programs examining their role. Today, PNG's politicians would love to have the same aura, but the huge turnover of MPs at each election (61 per cent in 2012) would indicate the people do not agree.

One of the difficulties that arose with the rapid transition from *kiap* rule to elected rule was the confusion it caused when power was being handed over even at a local council level. The young Australian *kiaps* were in charge of the police. They were magistrates with authority to hear court cases, hand down punishment and sentence people to jail. They could direct where roads were built and, when on patrol, they had health workers and agricultural officers under their command. The *kiaps* were the government. This became problematic when field staff started talking about transferring power to Papua New Guineans.

> Some village leaders thought they now had the authority of the *kiaps*: they could imprison, distribute funds and locate roads. But immediately they took any strong action, the *kiap* countermanded their orders. In their frustration and humiliation some village councillors shouted that they had been told a lot of lies.[22]

Australia may have presumed that the sort of Westminster democracy it bequeathed to PNG would work along similar lines to how it operates in Australia – although without the complication of a Senate, just a single chamber modelled on the House of Representatives. However, that is not how it has evolved. Among the many vast differences between Australia and PNG is that in Australia more than two-thirds of the seats in the House of Representatives are urban seats, while in PNG urban seats number just 8 out of 111. Another crucial difference is that politicians in PNG do not tend to regard themselves as 'representatives' of their people but rather as 'leaders' who are expected to deliver benefits directly to their constituents.

Winning a seat in the PNG Parliament creates enormous expectations and not just from the winner. The demands made on PNG MPs by their constituents would horrify any Australian politician. In many parts of PNG, the local member is regarded somewhat like the local ATM – and everyone, even those who did not vote for that member, has a special invisible ATM card that they expect their MP to honour. During the 1997 election campaign, I did a story for the ABC's *Foreign Correspondent* program that illustrated this only too well. We went to the electorate of Lagaip-Porgera in the Enga Province and spoke to the then sitting member, Anton Pakena. He told me that to have any chance of winning a seat, a candidate had to have vehicles. 'I'm running twelve vehicles on the road,' he said. 'All new ones. And you've got to feed the people – tinned fish, packet rice, coffee, sugar and so on. And you've got to give them money and so many things. If you don't give them the money they won't support you.'[23] He said his election campaign was costing him K600 000 (then about A$500 000).

One of Anton Pakena's supporters, Sol Taro, allowed us to film in one of his two shops. In the previous election, Sol had delivered his village's votes to Pakena and was showered with money from the public purse: K100 000 worth of vehicles, money for a church and K10 000 to start another business. With the refreshing frankness that is so typical of people in PNG, Sol was quite happy to tell me that the K10 000 grant never went to its intended purpose. His proposal for a new business was rejected, so he used up the money to buy beer and food for his large family. When I asked him why he supported Anton, he gave the revealing answer, 'Because he's a member and members hold the key to the money . . . I supported him and he bought me a truck. It's over there, a big Dyna.'[24]

Many years ago, I interviewed the then PNG Attorney-General, Bernard Narokobi, for a story about these expectations voters have of their elected member. He pulled from underneath his desk two large plastic bags filled with sheafs of paper. 'These are the requests for money from my constituents in the past few months,' he said. 'They want cash for school fees, bride-price payments, funerals, all sorts of things.'

The money that Anton Pakena was able to dispense back in Lagaip-Porgera in 1997 came from Electoral Development Funds. These funds, once disparagingly called 'members' slush funds', have had various names over the years. I asked Anton to take me to a project he had spent some of his money on. Much to my surprise he took me to inspect a complete failure. It was an egg production business. Inside the huge shed there were rows and rows of empty chicken cages, some covered by cobwebs. Discarded bags of chicken feed were scattered across the floor and empty cardboard egg cartons were everywhere. A tarpaulin draped over one end of the building flapped in the breeze. He'd donated K270 000 to this egg project but poor quality control and high prices meant it collapsed. When asked, he agreed the money had been wasted, adding: 'Not only on this project. But other projects too in this area.' It all seemed to be an incredibly frustrating waste, but he suggested that while it may have been embarrassing for the people he had helped, they were now in his debt and owed him their vote.

POOR DEVELOPMENT POLICIES

The money now going to members of the PNG Parliament to spend in their electorates has grown enormously. These days each member gets K15 million (A$7.5 million) a year: K10 million from the District Services Improvement Program (DSIP) which has fairly specific guidelines – 30 per cent to be spent on infrastructure, 20 per cent each on health and education, and 10 per cent each on law and justice, economic support and administration – and K5 million under another grant for additional investment in local health and education. This results in two main problems: first, the money is not always spent wisely, especially on the long-term maintenance of roads, airstrips and health centres; second, it inspires corruption. However, it does seem to have led to greater political stability, with MPs now devoting more of their time to organising the spending of these funds and less towards trying to engineer a toppling of the government. The current parliamentary term is likely to be only the second in the past forty years where the prime minister of the day has not been brought down and replaced mid-term.

Still, despite the guidelines, there is very little central control of the money that each MP receives. The Department of National Planning & Monitoring has almost no means of auditing whether the funds are actually spent as prescribed. Prime Minister Peter O'Neill contends that this spending in the members' electorates is transforming Papua New Guinea, enhancing political stability and bringing development to areas that have not been serviced for years. 'We are spending close to three billion Kina every year directly funding every district in the country,' he told a recent PNG Business Conference in Sydney. 'For the first time in forty years,' he went on, 'our communities are able to see the presence of government and the government's delivery of services.'[25]

Many people in PNG, however, question the effectiveness of the MPs' spending.[26] Dr Thomas Webster, a Western Highlander who headed up PNG's National Research Institute until mid-2015, says the huge amount of spending at the discretion of parliamentarians means that they have all become part of the executive arm of government. And he wonders what sort of a democracy PNG has become. 'In the Westminster system,' Webster says, 'you have the three independent accountability mechanisms of any state – the parliament that makes the laws and represents the people, the executive that runs the government with the public service and then you have the judicial services. At the moment in PNG there is no legislature – everyone is part of the executive arm of government. You have an executive government – the prime minister and all the ministers – and you have members of parliament, who are also heads of the district authorities, who are implementing projects and their main focus is that. They have sidelined the public service. So when they're involved in implementing there's no oversight. Who is going to do that oversight?'[27]

The MPs each chair their respective District Development Authorities and have considerable powers. Paul Barker, who runs the privately funded PNG think tank the Institute of National Affairs, says there is widespread cynicism about the way many MPs spend their K15 million each year. 'In some districts, it is being spent properly and a lot is coming out of it,' he concedes. 'But clearly in other districts there's little to show for it apart from perhaps real estate in northern Queensland or further afield these days as well.'

Barker says a lot of members have set up their own structures to administer the money. 'Many of them find it difficult to work with or refuse to work with the provincial administration,' he says. 'So the member sets up his own parallel mechanism to do the engineering designs and run other services. This parallel system by its very nature is not sustainable. They're not building up regular capacity. They're just bringing in a few people and at the next election if that person loses their seat then the new member will set up his team. But he's not going to maintain the things the previous member set up, so that then deteriorates. And if you have not had proper design and proper engineers and others to make sure things are done properly, the infrastructure and the public goods will probably just deteriorate rapidly anyway.'[28]

Prime Minister O'Neill defends the DSIP model, arguing that it is the district administrators who have the power to make sure the system works. He says that they, not the MPs, are the CEOs of the District Development Authorities. His model seems to be somewhat of a modified version of the old Australian colonial *kiap* structure, with the district administrator in charge of all government services in the member's electorate. O'Neill's father was a *kiap* who married into the Southern Highlands and stayed on in PNG after independence as a magistrate. 'It means transferring those staff at the district level to be accountable to the District Board rather than being accountable to Waigani,' O'Neill tells me.[29] (In PNG referring to 'Waigani', the Port Moresby suburb where most national government departments are based, has similar connotations to Australians disparagingly referring to 'Canberra'.) And O'Neill would like to see the process of devolving authority go even further. He wants police powers to be vested in the district administrator. And he wants that official to be in charge of all the other government employees as well, meaning they will supervise the work of teachers, doctors and nurses.

But Papua New Guinea's Auditor-General found major problems with how the DSIP funds were being spent. In an audit of twenty-two of the eighty-nine districts in 2012/13, more than K116 million (A$58 million) was spent on projects where expenditure was 'unsupported' by proper documentation or the projects were incomplete or abandoned. Over K39 million (A$19 million) was spent on non DSIP-related expenditure. Vehicles and heavy equipment with limited application towards DSIP objectives were bought at a cost of more than K58 million (A$24 million). And there was a 'significant under-spend' on water supply and sanitation, law and justice, rural communication and electrification, and health. The Auditor-General concluded that there had been 'limited value from the DSIP funds granted when measured against the original investment criteria', that there was a 'pervasive breakdown in the DSIP governance framework', and that 'better processes of accountability' were needed 'including the application of penalties for non-compliance'.[30]

CORRUPTION

At the end of April 2015, at least a dozen members of the PNG Parliament elected in 2012 had been charged with criminal or Leadership Code offences,[31] were awaiting sentence or had been jailed. Some of the cases were related to how DSIP grants were spent while others involved members of parliament abusing their powers. The longest prison term was twelve years.

During his relatively short term as prime minister of PNG, Sir Mekere Morauta introduced significant reforms that helped stabilise the political system and guaranteed greater independence of state institutions. He believes quite a deal of corruption in PNG is engendered by its particular form of democracy – the single member electorates that Australia imposed on PNG in the hope that the political system might work like it does in Australia. But the pressures on Australian MPs bear no comparison to those facing their PNG counterparts.

'The demand on members is for them to fund anything and everything,' Sir Mekere says. 'Members are not paid enough to satisfy those demands . . . and yet those demands are huge. And the only way they can satisfy those demands is to have access to public resources and abuse public resources. And there is a lot of temptation to make money on the side so that you can be a successful politician. Those pressures are very strong. And coupled with that is a lack of accountability, a lack of transparency, a lack of respect for process. Proper process is just not there. Anybody can do just about anything when you don't have to account for it. You don't have to take any notice of the Auditor-General. And if you are caught you just get a slap on the hand.'[32]

Perverse as it may seem, one of PNG's strengths is the amount of corruption that does get exposed. This is one area where Australia can look back with some satisfaction. Sir Hubert Murray did much in Papua between the wars to instil faith in an impartial justice system. He reviewed all court cases involving Papuans in every district station and personally signed the release papers of anyone he felt had been jailed unfairly. In the words of Ivan Champion, who worked in the Papuan administration, Murray constituted a 'court of appeal' for the local people. 'He didn't worry about Europeans; they could appeal somewhere else.'[33]

Sir Paul Hasluck argued that he wanted 'to familiarise' the indigenous people of PNG 'with the idea of justice as a principle to be applied without discrimination in all situations, the idea of law as a code that applied evenly and justly to all citizens, and the idea of courts of justice as institutions that were independent of, not subject to, the direction of those in authority.'[34] He succeeded. Papua New Guineans do see the courts as not being beholden to the government. Since independence, several Supreme Court rulings have gone against the government of the day. In 1994 Paias Wingti's government collapsed when the court ruled as unconstitutional his attempt to gain another eighteen months in power free from motions of no confidence by resigning in secret, springing that on a surprised parliament and then getting himself immediately re-elected.

The level and extent of the corruption that has been exposed is staggering. In March 2015, ACT NOW!, one of PNG's many vigorous non-government organisations (NGOs), held a mock 'birthday bash' to mark the fifth anniversary of the handing down of a damning report into PNG's Department of Finance. In its 827-page report, the Commission of Inquiry, headed by former justice Maurice Sheehan, found that K780 million (A$400 million) of public finances had been stolen between 2001 and 2006. At the mock party, the tables were covered with hundreds of cupcakes with the figure 'K5m' written in icing on the top. ACT NOW!'s Program Manager,

Effrey Dademo, told the crowd that no fewer than fifty-eight individuals including senior public servants and lawyers were recommended for prosecution by the police and the Ombudsman Commission. 'This birthday bash,' she said, 'is aimed at highlighting the irony that while the people of Papua New Guinea have suffered a huge injustice, those responsible for stealing money will be celebrating their continued evasion of justice and having a bash while the Inquiry recommendations are continually ignored.'[35]

The Chairman of Transparency International PNG, Lawrence Stephens, drew the attention of those at the party to the headline in one of the PNG newspapers the previous morning. 'It was on the front page: "K1.2 million was reported to have been stolen by a contractor falsely claiming to have done maintenance to toilets at the Boram Hospital in Wewak. An investigation has been called for." How often have we heard those words,' he asked, 'over how many years?' He said one item from the Finance Inquiry was the alleged illegal diversion of K1.3 million from the Sepik Highway Trust to a new but unrecognised university in Port Moresby. Although the Inquiry recommended that the Secretary of the Department of Finance be referred to the police, there was no evidence of an outcome.

ACT NOW! was established in 2010 as an advocacy group. Dademo was working as an environmental lawyer when she and others decided to set up their NGO. One of its main programs is titled 'Stop the Stealing', which focuses on the misuse of public funds in PNG. The group is determined to keep applying public pressure for action on corruption. 'The nature of debate in this country,' Dedemo says, 'is that one thing happens and everybody jumps up and says something and then they go quiet for the next ten years. So we're trying to keep the issues out there. We write blogs and encourage people through petitions and other online forums.'

In her address to that mock party, Dademo called on the government to keep its own promises on tackling corruption in PNG. 'In addressing a conference in Brisbane in August 2011,' she said, 'Prime Minister Peter O'Neill promised in no uncertain terms that his first challenge would be to fight corruption and abuse of public monies. He promised to establish an Independent Commission Against Corruption. He did set up an anti-corruption task force, which had been doing some brilliant work until it was disbanded. And when it was subsequently reinstated by the courts it was starved of vital funds to do its duties.'[36]

That anti-corruption unit is Task Force Sweep

and is headed up by a young lawyer, Sam Koim. It ran into trouble with the O'Neill government when Koim tried to have the prime minister arrested in relation to a major scandal involving huge payments to a law firm, Paraka Lawyers. Still, there had been some early successes, with ninety-one people arrested and charged. 'We've secured eleven convictions,' Koim told me. 'Four people are in jail – two members of parliament and two senior public servants. There have also been two suspended sentences. We have also recovered K214 million in tax – thanks to our inter-agency cooperative structure which enabled us to use various powers including tax powers.'[37] Some of that money has still to be paid. Koim listed another success as having been able to use the proceeds of crime legislation in Australia for the first time. That involved targeting properties in Cairns purchased with some of the ill-gotten gains.

LAW AND DISORDER

Crime is one of PNG's most difficult and perplexing problems. The crucial point about 'law' in traditional PNG society is that it was aimed at restoring balance to the community. It tended to be rough, it was ready, it was swift and it was not always fair. And some powerful men avoided it altogether. It also often involved compensation to the victims. The accused had few rights. Today things are different. As Paul Torato from PNG's Enga Province in the Highlands, who was PNG's Justice Minister for a time, puts it:

> Things have changed since we moved towards civilisation. In the Western kind of law, which we adopted, the offender is protected. They usually get away with it and the innocent are being victimised. But in our law, in our customs, we knew exactly who did it. Or we presumed who did it.[38]

But there is no single, agreed body of customary law. What held traditional society together were mechanisms and understandings that often varied significantly from place to place. What might quell feuding in one locality could be a recipe for conflagration in another.

The fact that more than 860 tiny, independent societies, each with its own interpretation of 'law', have been compressed into a modern nation state makes governing PNG extraordinarily difficult. The *kiaps*, who first brought the concept of a centralised government to the bulk of the people of PNG, subdued the fighting and introduced a veneer of harmony. But of all the colonial tasks performed by Australia, the establishment of a system of peaceful resolution had the most ephemeral results. The aims were high but the execution understandably confused.

The police force that Australia handed to PNG at self-government was particularly weak. A police department was not even created until the decade before independence. Up until then, the police had worked for the Australian administration's Department of Native Affairs. And in the year of independence, police responsibility covered only 10 per cent of the land area and 40 per cent of the population. A PNG policy document produced just one month after independence stated that the force faced 'major problems' because of inexperienced and untrained staff. 'Of a total force strength of 4400,' it said, 'there are 239 commissioned officers, 96 below established strength. Sixty-two officers are expatriates and 177 are Papua New Guineans.'[39] On average, the 177 PNG officers were aged twenty-eight and had been policemen for less than five years, and commissioned officers for less than three years. Worse were the severe shortages of senior non-commissioned officers. There were only 149 sergeants instead of the required 324; and only 306 senior constables when there should have been 575.[40] It was hardly the law enforcement agency one would wish upon a new nation with PNG's problems.

In 2014 the police force had 5700 officers.[41] While

the population of PNG had tripled since independence, the size of the police force had grown by just 30 per cent. The current police to population ratio is very low by world standards. At about 78 police per 100 000 people it is one-third of Australia's 268 police per 100 000. PNG's Melanesian neighbour, Vanuatu, has 277 per 100 000.[42] A report on trends in crime in PNG by the World Bank rated Port Moresby and Lae as two of the most dangerous cities in the world in 2010, based on 33 and 66 homicides per 100 000 persons, respectively.[43]

Tribal fighting in the Highlands remains a problem while migration to the cities adds to the tensions. A special report by the Australian Strategic Policy Institute on the future of Australia–PNG police cooperation says 'large fights, mainly over land issues that may go back decades, involve hundreds of warriors using military, high-powered and homemade guns' while intergroup clashes 'on the outskirts of cities and towns stem from friction as newer settlers from "outside" groups are blamed for taking work and causing crime'.[44]

Domestic violence is also a huge issue. In its 2015 World Report, the international NGO Human Rights Watch claimed PNG was 'one of the most dangerous places in the world to be a woman, with an estimated 70 per cent of women experiencing rape or assault in their lifetime'.[45] It noted that while domestic violence 'was specifically proscribed under the 2013 Family Protection Act, few perpetrators are brought to justice. Lack of access to courts and police, as well as failure by many justice officials to take violence against women seriously, contribute to the extremely low arrest and conviction rates.'[46]

Dame Carol Kidu served as PNG's Minister for Community Development for ten years, during which time she was the sole female member of parliament. She says the disturbing rate of violence against women is probably a product of the rapid transition PNG is going through and the clash of PNG's many cultures rather than being something that was normal in traditional society. 'Gender-based violence is almost portrayed as though this is cultural in PNG, that it is traditional – beating women to a pulp. I would never agree with that.'

Dame Carol, an Australian-born naturalised PNG citizen, fell in love and married the man who became PNG's first indigenous chief justice, Sir Buri Kidu from Pari village, close to Port Moresby. They met when he was a student in Queensland. 'I think Papua New Guineans have got to come to terms with what is culture and what is not,' she says. 'What is abuse of culture? Take bride-price. Traditionally it was protection for the woman if it was working properly.

Now it's terribly abused. We must come to terms with who we are and then work out how we can deal with this domestic abuse. I don't think we are taking control of the issues enough.'[47] She is right. PNG does need to address this issue of violence against women, particularly given the acute stresses PNG's rapidly changing economy and society are placing on families and relationships.

Sam Koim, a Highlander and the head of Task Force Sweep, agrees that the disconnection between trying to adapt to an introduced lifestyle and what was acceptable in traditional society may help explain the tensions that lead to violence. 'The missing link in all of this,' Koim tells me, 'is attitude! We have not emulated the Western culture we thought we were adopting. We have not held onto our traditional virtues and customs and values. In the process we got lost somewhere. Things like rape! I have never heard of rape in my own village. I have never heard of stealing in my own village. People stole from other tribes because we had tribal fights. But in the village stealing was taboo. If you steal or if you commit adultery with one of your brother's wives then you will be the first one to be killed. We have more social problems now than we had in those times.'[48]

PNG's strengths

It is easy to focus on PNG's weaknesses as a country. Less often do people consider its strengths. The economy is growing, the military has played a generally positive role, and although domestic violence and sexual aggression are real problems there are many remarkable PNG women who are making huge contributions to society. The country's physical beauty means that it has enormous potential as a tourist destination. PNG also has a vibrant and independent media that sheds much light on the country's problems, including corruption. This chapter will explore these and other more positive aspects of PNG life today.

ALMOST THE FASTEST-GROWING ECONOMY IN THE WORLD

In 2014 the Asian Development Bank predicted that

Papua New Guinea's economic growth for 2015 would exceed 21 per cent, making it the fastest-growing economy in the world. In early 2015 it revised that growth prediction downwards but still forecast that PNG's GDP would expand by 15 per cent.[49] PNG's central bank, the Bank of Papua New Guinea, was a little more cautious and in March 2015 it put the expected growth rate for the year at 9 per cent, partly because of falling gas and oil prices. Nevertheless, the central bank described 2014 as 'a milestone year' because revenue from PNG's first substantial liquefied natural gas (LNG) project had started to come in. That year was also PNG's fourteenth consecutive year of economic growth.[50]

Not surprisingly, Prime Minister Peter O'Neill has been upbeat about the country's economic performance. 'Papua New Guinea is entering a period of change never experienced before,' he told the Lowy Institute in an address in Sydney in May 2015. 'There are many contributing factors to this change. In large part, this can be found in the growth of our economy, the expansion of the middle class with new employment opportunities, and increasing disposable incomes that further feed business growth. As a result, there is a renewed hope and confidence amongst our people about the future of Papua New Guinea.'[51]

Australian investment in PNG is worth about A$19 billion while annual trade between the two countries amounts to about A$7 billion. Visiting PNG in May 2015 for the annual Papua New Guinea–Australia Business Forum, Australia's Minister for Trade and Investment, Andrew Robb, said the resources and energy sector was 'an area of growing collaboration', with Australia being a major supplier of equipment, technology and services to PNG's mining, oil and gas industries.

The PNG LNG project cost US$19 billion. ExxonMobil PNG is the project manager and largest shareholder, with about a third of the shares. The other joint venture partners are Oil Search Limited – a PNG-based company that is listed on the Australian Stock Exchange – which holds just under a third, with the rest shared between PNG government-owned entities, Santos Limited and Japan's JX Nippon Oil and Gas Exploration. Nine trillion cubic feet of gas will be shipped out of PNG over the thirty-year life of the project.

Oil Search is Papua New Guinea's biggest and most successful company. In September 2015, Woodside Petroleum made an A$11.6 billion takeover bid which Oil Search rejected. Any takeover would have to be approved by Prime Minister Peter O'Neill's government. Although O'Neill stated that he would like to speak to both boards, the price offered per share was well below what PNG itself paid when it bought back into Oil Search in 2014 under a complicated deal that earned the bank, UBS, a handsome commission.[52] Oil Search started looking for oil in PNG in 1929, although it took many years to make a profit.

With 95 per cent of Oil Search's assets located in PNG and more than 90 per cent of its staff Papua New Guineans, Oil Search's managing director, Peter Botten, is a firm believer in what he calls the company's 'social licence' to operate in PNG. 'As Oil Search's position in PNG grows,' he says, 'so is the commitment to putting something back into the broader PNG community.' For example, local landowner companies have received more than A$350 million in seed capital and contracts. Botten is frank about the reason: not only is it the right thing to do, he says, but it helps manage operating risks.[53]

Oil Search began working with the PNG Department of Health in 2007 to set up and manage HIV prevention and clinical treatment programs in previously neglected areas of the Highlands where it was operating. Since 2007 the company has supported the establishment of fifty-five new HIV testing sites. More than 30 000 people have been tested for HIV while more than 320 000 patients have been treated at medical centres supported by Oil Search. In 2011 Botten established the Oil Search Health Foundation, which now has seventy full-time staff. While Oil Search contributed almost A$11 million to the foundation, it has managed to attract grants to support its health work totalling nearly US$80 million.

The operators of the LNG project signed an agreement with the PNG Government to improve Port Moresby's sometimes erratic power supply. Under the agreement, up to 20 million cubic feet a day of natural gas will be supplied for twenty years to support government plans to improve the capacity and reliability of the country's power supply. Another 4 million cubic feet a day will also be provided for power generation in the Highlands.

Sir Kostas Constantinou, Chairman of Bank South Pacific and an Oil Search Board member for eleven years, says there is some concern about the downturn in world oil and gas prices, which would mean less revenue than expected going into the government coffers. It also means the government will need to readjust the budget and cut back on a number of projects. Still, he told me he is hugely optimistic about a second LNG project that involves the large French company Total. 'In this country, right now, we have another LNG project that is ready to go and in two years' time it will be ready for FEED [front end engineering design]. Tell me, where else in the world would you find that you have just finished one LNG project and things start to slow down and then it takes off again. And this second project could be the same size or maybe bigger than the Exxon one. PNG has a very good fiscal regime to do with oil and gas. Hence, Total and others are coming here. So the future, and I keep saying it, is great. In Australia they are winding back their LNG projects. Here, the next wave is happening. So there is a lot of blue sky.'[54]

The extra wealth has enabled Prime Minister Peter O'Neill to introduce a widely popular free education policy. That has been welcomed. However, the expectation that the government would reap considerable revenue from the exploitation of PNG's resources – not only from gas but also oil and minerals – has also led to an explosion in government spending. Paul Flanagan, a Visiting Fellow at the Development Policy Centre, Australian National University, says public debt levels by the end of 2015 were expected to skyrocket to 41 per cent of GDP. Revenues are down not only because of lower commodity prices but also because drought has forced the temporary closure of the Ok Tedi mine and proposed sales of government assets have not happened. 'Altogether,' he notes, 'revenues in 2015 are estimated to fall by K2546 million compared to the budget estimates, or 20.7 per cent of the government's own revenue base (excluding grants).'[55]

Flanagan's comments led to one headline suggesting that PNG faced a 'Greek-style' economic crisis.[56] But such a suggestion ignores the fact that unlike Greece, PNG has no burdensome welfare system and that the majority of the people of PNG are not totally reliant on a cash economy. They still have their own land, grow their own food, raise their own pigs and catch their own fish. The subsistence agriculture sector that feeds much of the population provides PNG with a fallback position that remains a great strength.

A DEVELOPING COUNTRY'S MILITARY WITH NO AMBITION TO RULE

In many other developing countries, the temptation for the military to remove fractious politicians and take control of the wealth generated by resource exploitation has proved irresistible. Certainly it is not an uncommon feature in PNG's broader neighbourhood. Yet in PNG the military has played a generally positive role. This was never better illustrated than by a now notorious incident that had its beginning in PNG's resource wealth.

Bougainville Copper Limited (BCL), which started

production in the early 1970s, helped underwrite Papua New Guinea's early years of independence. But in 1990 it became a casualty of what turned into a ten-year long secessionist war. The uprising began in 1988 as a landowner protest against environmental damage from the mine but fed into secessionist feelings that had simmered in Bougainville for decades. The war came to an end thanks to a most extraordinary series of developments that resulted in one of the defining events of PNG's first forty years of independence – the Sandline Affair.

By 1997 Prime Minister Sir Julius Chan was completely frustrated. He had tried peace talks on Bougainville that initially looked promising but failed. He had boosted funding to the Papua New Guinea Defence Force (PNGDF) to mount renewed assaults on the rebel-held heartland that never achieved their objectives. And he had set up a new provincial administration headed by a respected Bougainvillean jurist who was then murdered. So Chan and his finance minister, Chris Haiveta, turned to Sandline International. Sandline described itself as a company 'established to offer military consultancy and related services'. Its chief military man was Lieutenant-Colonel Tim Spicer, formerly of the Scots Guards, who had seen action in the Falkland Islands, Iraq in 1991 and in Bosnia.

Under a secret US$30 million deal, Spicer bought Russian military attack helicopters armed with high-explosive rockets, and Russian helicopter transports, and contracted the South African-based private military company, Executive Outcomes, to provide a mercenary force of Africans. The plan was for the mercenaries to train up the PNGDF's Special Forces Unit and then carry out a series of attacks to eliminate the leadership of the Bougainville Revolutionary Army (BRA). The principal figures behind Sandline had mining interests in Africa and intended to be involved in the planned reopening of the mine at Panguna once the military operation had crushed the BRA. The then Commander of the PNGDF, Brigadier General Jerry Singirok, led both Chan and Spicer to believe that he was in full support of the operation. However, he brought it all to an extremely swift end. He put Major Walter Enuma in charge of Operation *Rausim Kwik* – Melanesian pidgin for 'Get rid of them fast'. They captured Spicer and the Executive Outcomes leadership team, disarmed the mercenaries who had been training with the Special Forces Unit inland from Wewak in the East Sepik Province, and expelled them all from PNG. Spicer was kept in PNG for a short time to be questioned by a Commission of Inquiry that Singirok demanded be set up. Singirok had gone on national radio claiming the Sandline deal was corrupt. Public support for the PNG military was overwhelming.[57]

The current Commander of the PNGDF, Brigadier General Gilbert Toropo, was the officer in charge of the Special Forces Unit at the time and hosted the mercenaries. 'These guys came in with really crazy ideas and when I saw it I said, "This is not helpful for my countrymen . . . I am not going to go on a slaughtering operation." These guys who came from Africa didn't understand the nature of what our people are like. As Papua New Guinea Defence Force servicemen we knew who to target and who not to target. When we get someone from outside who comes in and they bring the weapons and they say they are going to solve it they would not know who is who. They would kill indiscriminately. And I told Jerry [Singirok], "These guys will do a lot of damage and go away. But you and I will have to deal with the catastrophe they create. And we will have to live with it all the rest of our lives." It would not look good. Jerry did the right thing in the best interests of Bougainville and the nation. The Bougainville crisis ended really because of the sending away of the Sandline mercenaries.'[58]

In 1999 I interviewed the then President of the Bougainville Autonomous Government, Joseph Kabui, who had been one of the key leaders of the secession movement. I asked him about the military rounding up and expelling the mercenaries and the public support in PNG that had attracted, and the impact that military operation had on Bougainville. 'It definitely helped the peace process,' he said, 'and it helped in a tremendous way really. Because it showed one thing – that the majority of people, the citizens of Papua New Guinea, were dead against a military option.'[59]

Prior to independence, Australia made a conscious effort to recruit soldiers from all around the country so that the Defence Force would not be dominated by a group from any one province or region. That has continued and the PNGDF prides itself on its contribution to national unity. 'I would like to think that the PNG Defence Force maintains that theme of building unity as a nation,' Toropo says. 'Of all the government institutions in PNG, I believe it is the Defence Force that has got beyond tribal and regional differences.'[60]

General Toropo says that the potential for tribal rivalries to cause problems in PNG institutions is real. But he says the PNGDF held together very well during the political crisis of early 2012 when Michael Somare and Peter O'Neill both claimed to be the legitimate prime minister. 'Back during that political impasse there was an attempt to break the fabric of that [PNGDF] unity,' Toropo says. 'But this organisation has a strong culture. If it was another organisation it could have resulted in a different scenario. But the PNG Defence Force is united. We don't operate along regional or tribal groupings. That is why we stood united.' At the time he was briefly put under house arrest by the faction supporting Somare. 'I was one of the victims,' he smiles. 'I was put under house arrest. But I put that aside and said, "Let's move on." This institution is too important for one or two individuals to take it down.'[61]

The only other comparable military force in the Pacific Islands region is in Fiji. There, the Fiji military has staged three coups – two in 1987 and one in 2006. During the Sandline crisis when Jerry Singirok captured and deported the mercenaries, he had a call from Fijian coup leader Major-General Sitiveni Rabuka, who asked him why he did not go all the way and take over the government. Singirok told him that was not the way the PNGDF operates. Toropo says he cannot see a military coup ever happening in PNG. 'I have said in many forums whenever this issue about the military taking over has been raised that in PNG it will not happen. Firstly, because the PNG Defence Force regards itself as a professional organisation and, secondly, with PNG made up of more than 800 different language groups and cultures, if anybody starts to cook up something, someone else will know about it and counter it. It will never happen. In fact, we are growing even further away from that possibility as the nation is developing.' And he makes this prediction: 'That view of the Defence Force being a threat to democracy here will eventually fade away.'[62]

RESILIENT WOMEN

A common image of PNG is that it is very hard on women. There is no denying that violence against women is a great problem, as discussed in the previous chapter. But focusing on this problem alone obscures the way in which women in PNG are making enormous contributions. It is the women of PNG who have traditionally been the workers. The men were the warriors. That is an oversimplification, of course, but it is true that many businesses in PNG find that female employees are more diligent and reliable. The Chairman of Bank South Pacific (BSP) says the bulk of the BSP branches are run by women. 'Why do we put women in charge?' Kostas Constantinou asks rhetorically. 'It's not just because they are females; it is because they are capable, they are organised, they are structured, they are firm and they are hard.' He says the future of PNG will be determined by the women. 'Let the women work, don't suppress them, give them opportunities, promote them and get more of them. The more women who get into parliament the better off PNG will be.'[63]

In the 2012 election just three women won seats. But that was a threefold increase on the previous parliament in which Dame Carol Kidu was the solitary female MP. And one of the women in particular made a significant breakthrough. Julie Soso defeated thirty-nine other candidates to become governor of the Eastern Highlands. (In PNG, the 111-member parliament is made up of eighty-nine members elected from individual constituencies throughout the country and twenty-two provincial governors elected by all the people in each of the provinces.) Soso became the first woman elected in any Highlands seat. The fact that she did it with votes from an entire Highlands province could be an indication of further changes to come. Titi Gabi, general manager of the online news service PNG Loop, says Soso's success is very encouraging, 'Especially in the Highlands where this big-man thing is really strong.'[64]

There are hundreds of PNG women with remarkable stories of how they have succeeded in what is generally regarded as a male-dominated society. Another example is Avia Koisen, who runs her own law firm in Port Moresby. But it took her a while to get there. 'Being the eldest of four girls and a Papuan from the Central Province I was only allowed to go up to Grade Ten,' she told a gathering at the Queensland Supreme Court's Banco Courtroom in July 2014. 'And then I was told that I couldn't go any further because I needed to work and support my three older brothers and four younger sisters and be a good girl, ready to be a good wife.' She ran away from home, studied nursing, then completed her High School Matriculation (Grades Eleven and Twelve) in one year, before going on to university and graduating with a Masters in Law from Queensland's University of Technology. After working for various government bodies and a bank for several years, she joined a private legal firm before launching out on her own.

'An opportunity arose when I was representing a couple of Papua New Guinean labourers who were employed by a [foreign-owned] logging company,' she told me. 'They were not paid for a few months so after a few letters of demand we ended up in the Labour Department.' The logging company's boss was there and initially refused to pay them, but Koisen would not leave until he did. 'In the end he paid. But at the same time he said to me, "Don't you work against me anymore. You come and work for me." So I said, "I don't want to work for you. I want to work for myself but if you will give me office space I will start. I will work for you pro bono but I will start having my own clients as well." So that's how it started – one desk, one computer,' Koisen laughed. 'And no car.'[65]

Avia Koisen has represented many women who have been subjected to domestic violence. And she says the policemen often side with the husband. 'There's one case where the client and I were being threatened with a gun. We were threatened to be thrown in the cell together. There's that general disrespect because we are women. And because our society is mostly patrilineal, men have the upper hand in most things.' Groups of women lawyers from Queensland and Victoria now provide training and mentoring for their female colleagues in PNG.

When I first went to work at the NBC of PNG in 1974 there was not a single Papua New Guinean woman in a senior management position. These days there are quite a few, including some who hold leading positions in the newsroom and others who manage some of the NBC's provincial radio stations. Back then, the parliamentary press gallery was almost totally male too. Today it is a very different situation, with female journalists among the top political and economic reporters.

TOURISM

While around a million Australians a year go to Bali for holidays, PNG attracts a bare 30 000 visitors. But when people do visit, the impact on them is often profound. As Lawrence Stephens recounts, 'When you get a member of your family who comes to visit you or when you run into a bunch of school kids who have walked the Kokoda Track or cycled down the Boluminski Highway in New Ireland and you hear them talking; or when you hear a bunch of Europeans who have just been backpacking through the Highlands using PMVs [locally owned Public Motor Vehicles – public transport] from Wabag to Lae and you hear their stories and how positive it all is – it's so annoying for PNG to have such a poor reputation when the few who come here know how fantastic it is.'[66]

Kevin Byrne, the former mayor of Cairns, who was born in PNG and headed up the PNG Tourism Office for several years, believes Papua New Guinea should have what he calls 'the most vibrant tourism industry in the world'. 'This would probably have to be the most gifted country with tourism assets,' he says. 'PNG is a very rich country. It has wonderful resources, wonderful people. We've got the best waters, we've got the best fishing and we've got the best reefs. It is amazing to go around the world and see countries promoting their own – and good luck to them – but I have been to most parts of the world and I can say unequivocally this is the most resource rich, gorgeous tourism destination in the world. The problem is always how do you manage those resources and make them accessible? How do you create a hospitality culture here? How do you say to the airlines or the government, "We have to have a transport system here that complements these resources? How do you make them accessible?"[67]

Ann Sherry, Chief Executive Officer of the holiday cruise company Carnival Australia, has a great enthusiasm for Papua New Guinea. P&O and Princess Cruises now visit seven ports in PNG. Not surprisingly, Port Moresby is not on the list. But some beautiful destinations are: Alotau, Doini Island, Kiriwina and Kitava Island are all in the Milne Bay Province, while the other three are Madang, Wewak and Rabaul. In April 2015, close to 600 guests on board the *Sun Princess* attended a special Anzac Day dawn service during a fifteen-night PNG cruise. It was a special event for one of those on board. Tom Iser was a World War II veteran who had served in PNG. He celebrated his ninety-sixth birthday during the cruise. 'Making the voyage back to Papua New Guinea brings back many memories of our fighting in the war there,' Iser is quoted by Princess Cruises as saying. 'But, of course, it is very different making the trip on a cruise and seeing the beauty of the islands.'[68]

FREE MEDIA

There is never any shortage of dramatic and interesting stories in PNG. In fact, there are enough stories for two daily newspapers in Port Moresby – *The National* and the *PNG Post-Courier*. And despite being available for free on the web, the papers hold their circulation and are airfreighted around the country.

The editor of News Corp's *PNG Post-Courier*, Alexander Rheeney, says the media has played 'a really critical role' in exposing what's gone wrong in PNG over the past forty years. 'We have a responsibility to this nation to continue to carry the torch and to hold government accountable,' he says. 'Freedom of expression and freedom of the press are pillars of our Constitution here in PNG. Every time a reporter signs a contract to join a newsroom, whether it's at the *Post-Courier*, *The National* or at a radio or TV station, they're basically signing a contract with the people of Papua New Guinea to get out there, to inform them, to educate them about the issues that the individual and ordinary Papua New Guineans are facing.'[69]

And, he believes, the public appreciate it. 'One of the beauties of social media since 2008 is that you can actually go online and you can see that support, you can read about it. Papua New Guineans are actually getting out there and expressing themselves and saying, "Thank you." And they're actually calling out the names of the individual reporters saying, "You've done a good job holding the government accountable in tackling, in exposing corruption!"' Rheeney says. One of the challenges that journalists now face is maintaining that trust with the people. 'We have to continue to do what we are supposed to do as reporters, to report without fear or favour. It is tough – but press freedom is alive and well in Papua New Guinea.'[70]

John Eggins, former news editor at the commercial television station EMTV, agrees. 'The media is one of the two fundamentals that hold democracy in this country together. The other, perhaps, is the judiciary. Freedom of the press is guaranteed by the Constitution, but the media can only be as good as the people in the industry. Unfortunately, a lot of experienced media personnel have moved on. But it is still vibrant. If you go back to the *Times of PNG* whose exposés of the forestry industry led to the Barnett Inquiry, and you look at the *Post-Courier* today – it is still reporting what some don't want reported. Same with *The National*. I just hope the journalists in the media these days are not being enticed by politicians and political parties to work for them.'[71]

Alexander Rheeney says a lot of his reporters come under pressure from both the government and the opposition. 'We have to try as much as possible to report objectively, to take the middle ground without fear or favour. We have to ensure we have both sides of the story. In almost every article that we publish, one side reckons that the other side should not have coverage at all!' he laughs. 'We have to educate our leaders about the role of the media and how it is important for us to have the other side of the story. A lot of Papua New Guineans, a lot of leaders, expect our reporting to put them in a good light all the time, not in a bad light. But we need to acknowledge the fact that there are issues, there are problems that Papua New Guinea continues to face and we need to acknowledge the problems that we face as a nation.'[72]

One of the newest competitors in the media in PNG is PNG Loop, an online news service owned by the Irish telecommunications company Digicel. Titi Gabi is the general manager. 'Our strength is really getting stories from the provinces,' she says. 'I started with twenty stringers and we've really established a good platform for provincial content. In PNG you need stories from outside the capital. But a lot of [the stringers] are in areas where there are difficulties logging on to the site. You have to be online to be consistent. But we are working on getting more [reporters].' She says connectivity is on the rise everywhere. 'It's improved hugely because Digicel has gone out to greenfield sites and they have put up about 300 new towers connecting some really remote areas. There are new towers in Bougainville and the Highlands so connectivity has really improved.'[73]

I asked Gabi about the public reaction to PNG Loop. 'It's a mixed bag really. Those who understand what online news is welcome it. Many others think we're just a Facebook news organisation because we have a Facebook page and share our stories on there. The statistics so far show that 90 per cent of our readers gain access via Facebook. What I have heard lately is good stuff, compliments. People saying, "You are providing a service that PNG should have had years ago."'[74]

Gabi says intimidation is a factor she and her reporters have to contend with. 'A lot of the censorship is self-censorship because of the threats of intimidation from outside. It influences the style of writing, how much people want to say,' she says. 'It is not healthy. It is not good. Work needs to be done in that area.'[75] Nevertheless, Kostas Constantinou says the PNG media is getting stronger. 'You read the letters to the editor, you see the front pages – anyone can condemn a politician without fear. Look at the rest of the world, look at some of these African states, you get up and say something and you will know about it but not for long because you will be six foot under. I say to people when I am travelling overseas and they ask what is PNG like? "The greatest thing about PNG is the freedom of the press!"'[76]

Why Australia needs
to re-engage

Julie Bishop must have been tearing her hair out. The Federal Budget for 2015/16 had just come down and she had protected Papua New Guinea from the most savage cuts to Australia's aid spending. While the total aid budget was slashed by 20 per cent, the bilateral aid Australia gives to PNG was cut by only 5 per cent, or A$25 million. Still, at A$477 million it was not much below half a billion dollars. When PNG's share of regional and global aid programs and other assistance is included, the total aid to PNG comes to A$554 million. Bishop had ensured that PNG returned to being the largest single recipient of Australian aid, following a massive cut of 40 per cent to Indonesia's share (down from A$605 million to A$375 million).[77]

But what was grabbing the headlines in PNG and

giving Bishop grief was PNG's fury at the simultaneous announcement that Australia was establishing a diplomatic post in Bougainville. 'We were shocked,' PNG's Prime Minister Peter O'Neill told the Lowy Institute two days after the budget was brought down. 'As we all know, Bougainville is an integral part of Papua New Guinea and there are clear historical sensitivities around Bougainville that must be appreciated.' The announcement came while new elections for the Autonomous Bougainville Government were underway. 'There has been no consultation on this proposal,' O'Neill said, 'and there is no agreement to proceed. As we respect the territorial integrity of others, we expect others to respect us as well.'[78]

Papua New Guinea's Foreign Minister, Rimbink Pato, banned Australians from travelling to Bougainville, calling the announcement of the proposed diplomatic post 'outrageous' and 'mischievous'. 'I have instructed the chief migration officer to impose the ban with immediate effect,' Minister Pato said, adding that airlines operating flights to Bougainville would also be notified not to allow Australians on board.[79]

How could this have happened? Is it just another example of Australia's insensitivity and lack of any real understanding of our former colony? The

Foreign Minister's office in Canberra said Bishop had raised the issue during a visit to Papua New Guinea in December 2014. But in Port Moresby the memory is more about her proposal to set up a post in PNG's second city and major industrial hub, Lae. That proposal never made it into the Australian budget, while the Bougainville post did, leaving the impression that Australia was getting ready to recognise an independent Bougainville. This episode is symptomatic of many of the things that are currently wrong with Australia's relationship with PNG. How could Australia mess up the simple job of getting approval from PNG's leadership about a consulate opening?

As the last two chapters have highlighted, PNG has its share of problems, but it also has its strengths. As the former colonial power Australia has a responsibility to help PNG deal with its challenges, some of which result from Australian policies of the colonial era. But the country is far from being a basket case. In the forty-two years since I first set foot in PNG, I have seen it make significant progress, often with the help of aid and development cooperation from Australia. If this is to continue, however, and if the bilateral relationship is going to deliver strong mutual benefits, then Australia will need to re-engage deeply and broadly with its nearest neighbour.

BUILT ON AID

With 360 staff, Australia's high commission in Port Moresby is larger than our embassy in Washington. The reason we have so many staff in Port Moresby is because of the size of Australia's aid program in PNG. We need to ask, however, how well is that half a billion dollars of Australian taxpayers' money being spent and what impact is the spending of that aid having on the quality of our relations with PNG?

At independence and for some years after, Australian aid to PNG was provided as a cash grant to the PNG budget, to be spent as PNG saw fit. These days there is no cash component left. It is all tied to specific programs and projects that are overhauled and changed regularly – particularly when there is a change of government in Australia.

Just how effective the Australian aid is remains one of the great conversation topics in PNG. 'The "barbecue stopper" here,' says Kevin Byrne, the former head of PNG Tourism and long-time resident of PNG, 'is essentially how ineffective the aid program has been.' Byrne also notes a general disregard that the Australian Department of Foreign Affairs and Trade seems to have towards any Australians who have had a long association with Papua New Guinea. 'You've had a long association, Sean. I have. And a number of other people have. This is a very worthwhile resource for these Australian Foreign Affairs aid programs to tap into. But there is a disdain. There is this attitude that, you're an old-time Aussie Papua New Guinean. You are irrelevant. You have this colonial ego and we are all about the new paradigm in Australia's dealings with Papua New Guinea.'[80]

In one conversation I had with Australian High Commission officials in Port Moresby while preparing this Paper, I was admonished for 'thinking like a Papua New Guinean'! While it must be admitted that race relations in the colonial era between some Australians and Papua New Guineans were sometimes fraught, most of the Australians who decided to remain in PNG or who have spent a considerable number of years there have wonderful connections and deep friendships with the people. And they know how the country operates. This does not mean they are smarter than Australian officials who have just arrived. But it does mean that they could be a valuable source of advice. There seems to be an unfortunate attitude among some in Canberra that not only are all Papua New Guineans corrupt, but any Australians who live in the country and love it are somehow tainted as well.

Back in 1997 an Australian Government briefing paper for the then treasurer, Peter Costello, was left on a coffee table during the South Pacific Forum Economic Ministers' Meeting in Cairns. A Reuters journalist picked it up and published its contents, which revealed in colourful language Australia's disparaging view of PNG. It also provided a character assessment of PNG's then deputy prime minister and minister for finance, Chris Haiveta, who was attending the meeting, that was not only insulting but in some respects quite wrong. Professor Edward Wolfers, who has worked closely with PNG's Department of Foreign Affairs for many years, wrote in the *Sydney Morning Herald* at the time that the 'dismissive, almost contemptuous way in which the brief described regional leaders' was indicative of an attitude long suspected by those who have to deal with Australian officials. 'Anyone who has attended official hearings and presentations on Australian aid to Papua New Guinea must have observed the increasing disregard for local sensitivities displayed by Australians who criticise conditions there,' he wrote, 'including alleged corruption and mismanagement.'[81]

When I asked former prime ministers Chan and Morauta what they thought of the aid program, all I heard was exasperation. Sir Julius Chan, who had been PNG's finance minister at the time of independence, believes that the switch in aid to a host of programs and projects led to 'a very cumbersome, very tedious, very unnecessary load of work' for PNG's bureaucrats. And he said that at the time of the Sandline crisis, John Howard threatened to withdraw aid. 'I began to dislike some of the policies of Australia,' he told me. 'When aid is tied there is the prerogative to take it away. So my relationship [with Australia] turned sour.'[82]

Sir Mekere Morauta said he had given up trying to give advice. 'I have become very uninterested in talking to Australia because nothing happens!' He said Australian aid used to be 'extremely important' to PNG. 'It still is important. But in my days as secretary for finance we had a very strong Treasury and very strong Planning Office. Treasury and Planning worked very, very closely. When it came to the use of Australian aid or other aid, our approach was that everything went through the budget, the development budget. And aid donors were told, "If you want to give your aid then this is the shopping list. It has been approved by the parliament. These are our priority projects [and] you pick what you want to fund from there." And it worked perfectly well because money was spent on our priorities, government-approved priorities. What has tended to happen now is that our lack of coordinating with our budget has left our aid donors really worried we are not spending anything properly, so they are now spending it themselves.'[83]

PNG has not done itself any favours by the way it has spent some of its own money, for example paying out millions of dollars to a legal firm for work in prisons the government was told it was getting for free. There have been instances, too, where Australia has pulled money out of an aid program because of alleged corruption. In December 2013, Australia withdrew A$38 million from a program supplying medicine to PNG's 3000 health centres when it was found that the company that won the tender, Borneo Pacific, had not only bid A$9 million more than the company that had successfully delivered the kits previously but also did not have the internationally recognised quality control certification previously required.[84]

While there are obvious problems on the PNG side, another factor that undercuts the effectiveness of our aid is the constant turnover of our aid officials at the high commission. Dr Thomas Webster, who headed PNG's National Research Institute until mid-2015, says he has wasted a lot of time trying to educate Australian aid officials. 'I've been here ten years and I've talked to probably five or six streams of young people who've come to work on PNG aid. And they come and say, "What do you think about this?" And I talk to them, I engage with them and I think they've developed an understanding and then they move on and another person comes in and I begin again talking to them. So they really don't understand the needs.'[85] He believes this means they fall back on the latest international aid theories, which themselves seem to change regularly.

Webster also says PNG government officials don't bother to contest the latest theories, not only because they know the Australians they are dealing with won't be around for very long but also because they're not inclined to discuss the priorities for aid programs with people who don't know the issues. 'Government officials don't go out of their way to be very critical of people who don't have a clue and so if they're asked, "Are these your problems?" They say, "Maybe?" We Papua New Guineans don't engage in a debate or a discussion as to whether there are other things that would be more appropriate. So in this environment, aid has not been effective! Not as effective as it should have been because we have not had that robust debate and solid discussions with people with a depth of experience.'[86]

THE SECURITY IMPERATIVE
Way back in 1950, former Australian Prime Minister Billy Hughes spoke on the ABC's *Guest of Honour*

radio program about how, at the Paris Peace Conference after World War I, he had 'fought for the mandate over New Guinea and the adjacent islands, control of which,' he said, 'was vital to the very existence of Australia as a free democracy.' He said that when the British Prime Minister, Lloyd George, who opposed Australia getting control of the former German colony, said the Royal Navy would not help Australia keep possession of it, he challenged him to a debate on the issue before the British people who owned the Navy. 'And when Lloyd George turned away in anger at my plain speaking,' Hughes said, 'I gave up speaking in English and told him in Welsh – a fine language for invective – just what I thought of him.' Hughes finished this tale by saying that in getting the mandate Australia 'gained command of a bastion which in the hands of an enemy would almost certainly have meant irreparable disaster in the last war'.[87]

Japan was given a post-WWI League of Nations mandate over most of Micronesia to PNG's north. The former German colonies – in what are now the Federated States of Micronesia, Palau, the Marshall Islands and the Commonwealth of the Northern Mariana Islands – became Japanese-mandated territories. As Hughes indicated, if Japan had administered New Guinea through the 1920s and 1930s,

Australia would have been in a lot more trouble than it already was at the beginning of the war in the Pacific.

PNG remains prominent in Australian security thinking. Australia's 2013 Defence White Paper lists a 'secure Australia' as our top strategic interest, then continues:

> Our next most important strategic interest is the security, stability and cohesion of our immediate neighbourhood, which we share with Papua New Guinea, Timor-Leste and South Pacific states. Australia seeks to ensure that our neighbourhood does not become a source of threat to Australia and that no major power with hostile intentions establishes bases in our immediate neighbourhood from which it could project force against us.[88]

PNG's security and prosperity are hugely important for Australia. It is our nearest neighbour – in fact, three Australian islands in the Torres Strait are just off the southern coast of PNG and lie in three tiny, excised areas of Australia that are actually inside PNG's 12 mile (22.2 kilometre) territorial seas. Papua New Guinea's population is also growing rapidly and there are some predictions that if it continues unabated, PNG could have the same population as Australia by 2050. That rapid population growth could exacerbate frictions that already exist between people from different regions within the country. When the ethnic war in Solomon Islands led to a request from that country's parliament for Canberra's help, Australia ended up spending A\$2.6 billion on the ten-year long Regional Assistance Mission to Solomon Islands (RAMSI).[89] Australia will also have to consider the uncertain future of Bougainville. The people of Bougainville are being given the opportunity to vote on whether they want to break away from PNG in the next few years. But any separation would have to be approved by the PNG Parliament, a most unlikely development. And what then?

As Paul Barker from PNG's Institute of National Affairs notes, it is critical for Australia that PNG as an economy and as a democratic society works. 'If PNG works,' he says, 'then Australia has a very good neighbour with a lot of affluent citizens who can be trading with Australia, holidaying in Australia and vice versa. Hopefully it can be a law-abiding and peaceful society. But if it doesn't work, if governance implodes, if the benefits from the resources raise aspirations but at the same time raise levels of disappointment because fulfilment doesn't come out of it all and money is misused, diverted or misappropriated, then on Australia's doorstep you are going to have a very problematic country. And that would be a dangerous country for Australia.'[90]

POLITICAL INDIFFERENCE

Foreign Minister Julie Bishop is genuinely interested in PNG. But there is little knowledge or understanding of PNG among many other members of the Australian Parliament. Kevin Rudd as prime minister made a good start in giving PNG some recognition. His first overseas trip as Prime Minister was to PNG and then he went on to Solomon Islands where Australia was funding RAMSI. Julia Gillard made one trip to PNG. The significance of that was described by Jonathan Schultz, a researcher in political science at the University of Melbourne, as lying 'in the symbolism of a prime minister facing almost certain imminent electoral defeat paying a visit to a country that, for all its strategic, economic and humanitarian importance, receives only sporadic attention from Australian governments'.[91]

When Rudd returned as prime minister, that sporadic attention gained a new central focus – asylum seekers. Rudd resurrected the Howard-era 'Regional Processing Centre' in the Manus Province by getting PNG Prime Minister O'Neill to agree that Papua New Guinea was such a dreadful place that sending asylum seekers to Manus could solve Australia's boat people problem. The cash incentives certainly helped O'Neill decide. Australia agreed to a range of multi-million dollar funding initiatives including half the costs of a new, modern base hospital in Lae, a major upgrade of the Lae-Madang highway and the provision of fifty Australian police to assist in the training of the Royal PNG Constabulary.

The deal was greeted with some dismay in parts of Papua New Guinea. '[It's] going back to the World War II syndrome that Papua New Guinea is the frontline,' said Paul Barker from the PNG Institute of National Affairs. 'It's not a popular initiative.' Barker said the asylum seeker problem was seen in PNG as 'an Australian problem and why should Australia export its problems to PNG?'[92] While there has been some employment created on Manus and a few business opportunities there is real annoyance within the host province that many of the extra aid benefits went to the mainland.[93] Assimilating the mostly Muslim people who are classified as genuine refugees into PNG's strongly Christian communities adds yet another challenge for a country with no shortage of challenges already.

Labor's then foreign minister, Bob Carr, hailed the Manus agreement as a 'masterstroke'.[94] Yet a year earlier, Carr had threatened to mobilise the world against Papua New Guinea when there was a suggestion that PNG's elections, due in 2012 at the expiry of the regular five-year term, could be delayed by a year. 'You've got Australia placed in a position where we'd have no alternative but to organise the world to condemn and isolate Papua New Guinea,' Senator Carr told Sky News. 'We'd be in a position of having to consider sanctions.'[95]

I was stunned when I heard this. Carr obviously thought he needed to send a strong warning but for anybody who understood what was going on in PNG it was totally unnecessary. There was no way the elections were going to be shelved. The proposal to delay the election had come from PNG's then deputy prime minister, Belden Namah. But Carr's advisers on PNG should have known that Namah and Prime Minister Peter O'Neill, never close, were in a union of temporary convenience. O'Neill was actually looking forward to the election in the expectation, which proved correct, that he could dump Namah in the aftermath. So the threat to organise the world to condemn and isolate PNG and impose sanctions simply revealed a shallow understanding of PNG's politics.

Back during the height of the Sandline mercenaries drama, which led to public protests and some looting in Port Moresby, Australia's then shadow foreign minister, Laurie Brereton, earned himself condemnation in *The National* when he suggested that all Australian Defence Force staff in Port Moresby should take refuge in the Australian High Commission. 'It was all in the great tradition of the famous headline in *The Rabaul Times*,' *The National* claimed, 'that trumpeted "No White Woman Safe!", after a minor incident in that town. The headline was published in 1929, and much of Mr Brereton's explosive rhetoric belongs in the same era.'[96]

A SHRINKING MEDIA PRESENCE

It is easy to blame officials and politicians for our poor engagement with PNG. But the problem is much broader than that. As I noted at the outset of this Paper, few Australians seem to care or even know very much about their former colony. One of the reasons is that the Australian media generally ignores PNG. Flick through your average daily newspaper and the international news is dominated by date lines from North America, Europe or the Middle East. There is little news from southern hemisphere capitals, and certainly not from Port Moresby.

When I first went to PNG in 1974, there were six Australian journalists based in Port Moresby reporting for Australian news outlets. The ABC had two while the Fairfax newspapers (*The Age* and the *Sydney Morning Herald*), Australian Associated

Press (AAP) and the *Herald and Weekly Times* each had their own correspondents and there was a free-lancer who earned a decent living servicing weekly newspapers and other media organisations. PNG was on the verge of independence and there was some expectation it could result in chaos and mayhem. In fact, PNG had a very peaceful transition to independence and the Australian media rapidly lost interest. When I became the ABC correspondent in PNG in 1979 there were still four Australian journalists reporting news to Australia. But the Fairfax newspapers pulled out in 1980 and the *Herald and Weekly Times* in 1981. A few months before that last newspaper correspondent left, we had a discussion on news values and he told me he knew what the subeditors at the *Melbourne Herald* wanted. 'They want *raskols*, plane crashes and tribal fights! And that's what I'm giving them.'

So from 1981 it was down to just two Australian journalists reporting on PNG – one at the ABC and one at AAP. Then in 2013, AAP closed its bureau in Port Moresby, which had been operating for almost sixty years. The ABC correspondent is the solitary member these days of the PNG Foreign Correspondents' Club. Alexander Rheeney, the news editor of the *PNG Post-Courier*, says he cannot understand why the Australian media has so little interest in a country that gets more than half a billion dollars of Australian taxpayers' money, where Australian investments total A$19 billion and two-way trade is worth A$7 billion. 'That was tragic,' he says reflecting on the closure of the AAP bureau. 'We've always had the ABC around here but I thought having AAP around and the fact that it represented the commercial side of the media in Australia was a bonus. It's even more difficult now for PNG-related stories to get a run in the mainstream media in Australia. Having AAP in Port Moresby enabled PNG stories to get straight into the newsrooms in Sydney or Brisbane or Melbourne. Now we don't have that link.'[97]

Titi Gabi from the online news service PNG Loop says the overseas correspondents have provided more than just a service to the Australian media. 'The foreign correspondents here provided a balance for us,' she says. 'I am a Papua New Guinean. I have those daily struggles that culturally you can't do or say this and this and this. But the foreign correspondents can. And with AAP gone, who is telling our stories in Australia now? PNG is the largest Pacific Island nation. Australia spends a lot of money on PNG. It just does not make sense.'[98]

Her concern is shared by John Eggins, the former news editor at EMTV, who says that although

EMTV was owned by Australia's Channel Nine, up until a few years ago there was next to zero interest in Channel Nine taking any news stories from his newsroom. 'Channel Nine was here for a commercial purpose,' he says. 'It was not interested in what was going on between Canberra and Port Moresby.'[99]

The Post-Courier is owned by News Corp but Alexander Rheeney says there is not much interest in the Murdoch newspapers in Australia taking advantage of the fact that they have a newsroom full of PNG reporters in Port Moresby. 'I do liaise with our colleagues from our sister papers down in Australia on PNG-related stories,' he says. 'But a lot of it is on crime.'

Rowan Callick, Asia Pacific editor at *The Australian*, is one of the few journalists left in the mainstream print media in Australia with any detailed knowledge and experience in PNG. Callick lived in PNG for ten years and worked for Word Publishing, which is jointly owned by the major Christian churches. Word Publishing produces the Melanesian pidgin newspaper, *Wantok*. While working there, Callick started up what was for a long time a top-quality weekly English language newspaper, *The Times of PNG*, which broke many corruption stories and prompted a comprehensive inquiry into the logging industry. Another Australian journalist who takes a real interest in Papua New Guinea is Jo Chandler, who wrote some excellent stories for the Fairfax papers before they lost interest and made her redundant. Chandler is now operating as a free-lance journalist. Some of her stories have appeared in *The Guardian* online and she wrote a major piece on violence against women in PNG for the Lowy Institute.[100]

The reluctance of Australia's mainstream media to take PNG seriously leads to some resentment. Some years ago, *The National* ran an article criticising the Australian media for ignoring the region of the world where Australia is geographically based. 'Part of the Australian media's blindness,' the PNG news-paper argued, 'stems from that country's apparent endemic identity crisis. Who are the Australians? Are they a lost tribe that has strayed from its ethnic and cultural roots in distant Britain and Europe?'[101] On Bob Carr's one trip to PNG as foreign minister, he travelled to the Highlands with his PNG counterpart. Both were carried into the PNG minister's village on a decorated platform, held on the shoulders of twelve men. Senator Carr was presented with a pig and one of the Australian journalists travelling with him wrote about it, prompting the *Sunday Herald Sun* to run the headline: 'How some cannibals, a throne and a hairy pig won over Foreign Minister

Bob Carr'.[102] It is that sort of headline that causes great offence in PNG.

'We have got to understand that PNG is looking towards moving closer to China and closer to Indonesia,' says Kevin Byrne, the former head of PNG Tourism. 'Unless we as Australians manage this era well and manage it practically we will lose it. We will lose it and we will become a footnote on the history of Papua New Guinea unless we as Australians identify what the issues are and go at them in a cooperative, friendly and respectful way.' He says he dislikes the term 'brothers' that Tony Abbott once used to describe Australians and Papua New Guineans. 'We are not brothers! We are "great mates".'[103] If we are to retain that mateship, then the Australian media needs to re-engage and take a genuinely serious interest in covering events in Papua New Guinea.

What should
be done?

Richard Marles, Shadow Minister for Immigration and Border Protection, says he believes Australia has a moral obligation to take Papua New Guinea more seriously. 'It is one of the two countries in the world that got its independence from Australia,' he says. The other one is Nauru, which Australia has also turned into an offshore asylum seeker processing centre. 'Papua New Guinea is our nearest neighbour,' Marles says. 'It is 50 per cent bigger than New Zealand. It fits integrally into our national security framework, which is evidenced by our own military experience up there during the Second World War. Can there be a more sacred site than Isurava and the Bomana War Cemetery and the Kokoda Track? PNG is the custodian of all that. It is the place of our largest aid program. It's our largest overseas mission.

It just deeply, deeply matters.'[104]

The 2015 Lowy Institute Poll shows that 77 per cent of Australians agree that Australia has a moral obligation to help PNG and that 82 per cent believe stability in PNG is important to Australia's national interest.[105] In this Paper I have argued that while Papua New Guinea has its challenges, it is not a hopeless case. Australians need to move beyond this corrosive belief that no amount of Australian aid money will fix PNG's problems or that nothing good can come out of a deeper engagement with our former colony.

Just sixteen years after PNG's independence, in 1991, the Australian Parliament's Joint Committee on Foreign Affairs, Defence and Trade conducted an inquiry into Australia's relations with Papua New Guinea. The Committee's 269-page report began with a statement that would not have been out of place in this Paper's introductory chapter:

> Australia's relationship with Papua New Guinea is governed by the fact that we obtained it as a colony in a burst of strategic nervousness just as we ourselves were seeking decolonisation. We were, therefore, diffident colonisers who governed with casual practicality and who departed with alacrity and too little care.[106]

The Committee concluded that the Australia–PNG relationship had by then already been 'weakened . . . especially at the individual level'; that 'Papua New Guineans know much more of us than we know of them'; and that the 'fault lies particularly with Australians'. The report went on to note:

> Apart from those people whose connections with Papua New Guinea go back to pre-independence days and the small group of officials who deal with the relationship at an official level, there are few in Australia who know or understand Papua New Guinea well. Papua New Guinea does not figure in Australian school curricula, there are few cultural, sporting or tourist links and the media in Australia presents a narrow and sensationalised view of Papua New Guinea as a violent and disintegrating society.[107]

Ian Kemish, Australia's high commissioner in PNG from 2010 to 2013, is one of those whose connections go back to pre-independence. In an address to the Griffith University's Perspectives: Asia lecture series at the conclusion of his term, he regretted that there was 'a blind spot' in Australia about PNG. Kemish spent a lot of his childhood in Papua New Guinea and at the end of the lecture I asked him to explain his 'blind spot' comment. 'Well, it's a paradox,' he said. 'There are so many Australians who belong to the same tribe as me – people who have an extraordinary level of personal connection with the country, people who grew up there, people whose ancestors fought there in the Second World War, people who have modern-day connections. That all exists and there are Australians who have quite deep knowledge and, by the way, affection for PNG. But there is still in some quarters a surprising lack of knowledge about a country which lies less than 4 kilometres from the northern-most Queensland islands. There is a bit of a paradox there and I think there's a responsibility for all of us to think about and talk about what is happening in Papua New Guinea a bit more.'[108]

There are a number of initiatives governments, the media, business and academia could pursue, both in Australia and PNG, to revitalise the relationship between our two countries. Indeed, some of the recommendations from the 1991 Joint Parliamentary Committee report are worth following up, a quarter of a century after they were made.

One idea from the Joint Committee report was that there should be alternating yearly visits by delegations of parliamentarians from either country. As noted earlier in this Paper, the level of knowledge among Australia's MPs is poor. As the Committee suggested, the presiding officers of the two national parliaments could formalise, by agreement, links between backbenchers from both countries. It might also be worthwhile if the major political parties in Australia examined how they might develop relationships, even informal ones, with the significant political parties in PNG. For example, members of the Australian Labor Party and the New Zealand Labour Party know each other well, as do some of those in the Australian Liberal Party and the National Party in New Zealand. Admittedly, the backgrounds of those parties are similar.

RETHINKING THE AID RELATIONSHIP

There is no question that if we are to improve the quality of the relationship between Australia and PNG we need to rethink the aid relationship. This is, of course, easier said than done, and has already been attempted a few times. But especially in light of changes in the PNG economy, it needs to be done again. A particular focus has to be increasing the capacity of PNG government officials, rather than simply implanting Australian officials in the PNG bureaucracy because we do not think their officials are up to the task.

Prime Minister Peter O'Neill earnt himself some

shrill headlines in Australia in August 2015 following a statement on how he believed the aid relationship could improve. He was said to have plans to 'boot out Australian officials' working for his government and that he would 'turf out all foreign advisers by the year's end'.[109]

The full statement, in fact, should be welcomed by Australia as it indicated a determination by PNG to take greater control of tackling its problems. 'As a developing country we don't want handouts,' O'Neill said, 'we don't want Australian taxpayer money wasted and we don't want boomerang aid.'[110] His complaint was about how much money never reached its real purpose. 'Development assistance has become a billion dollar "industry" where so much of the goodwill ends up in the pockets of middlemen and expensive consultants,' he said. 'I wonder if the people of Australia realise how much of the money they give to help Papua New Guinea and other countries is actually paid to middlemen and lawyers.'[111] He said that rather than having advisers who worked for their own governments he wanted to move to a model in 2016 'where our partners will be welcome to fund positions within our government. These staff can then work and report through the Papua New Guinea government system and we will deliver their salaries through arrangements with the donor countries.'[112] He predicted this would help strengthen PNG's government systems from within and gradually wean PNG off development assistance.

O'Neill also forecast a change to the policing assistance given by Australia. 'We have had a policing partnership program in place for a couple of years now and I think all parties agree, the benefits are limited due to restrictions placed on the Australian police. We have Australian police officers who are committed to strengthening law enforcement in our country, but they are frustrated by the bureaucracy that means they cannot do hands-on policing. I cannot imagine being a police officer who is told that if they see a crime being committed, he or she has to stand back and watch. We would like to recruit foreign police into line positions within the Royal Papua New Guinea Constabulary so they can lead by example and pass on their knowledge and skills.'[113]

There are signs that the government is shifting to a greater focus on capacity. Foreign Minister Julie Bishop has pushed for the creation of a Pacific Leadership and Governance Precinct in Port Moresby to improve the training of PNG public servants. Back in the colonial era, Australia had a highly regarded training institute in Sydney called the Australian

School of Pacific Administration (ASOPA). It ran tertiary level courses for people recruited to work in PNG, including the *kiaps* and teachers. In 1970 it started training Papua New Guineans when Australia realised there was going to be a serious shortage of well-trained and qualified indigenous people to replace the Australians. My sister-in-law spent ten months there in the mid-1970s doing a management training course. This new Governance Precinct that Australia is funding is, in some ways, ASOPA resurrected. The aim is to build leadership and management skills across all levels of the PNG public service. In a press release issued for the launch of the Precinct in November 2015, Julie Bishop said, 'The institutions involved in the Precinct will work closely with the public and private sector to foster the ethical, practical and intellectual framework to help build the leadership qualities and skills of government officials.'[114]

YOUNG LEADERS' EXCHANGES

A small start has already been made in trying to develop better connections between young leaders in both countries. Some formal exchanges have begun, thanks to the support of both the Australian and PNG governments. Australia has provided funding that enables the Lowy Institute to host a regular Emerging Leaders'

Dialogue through its Australia–PNG Network. Ten young leaders from each country and from a variety of sectors are brought together each year to discuss potential collaboration. I was invited to the dialogue session in December 2014 and came away extremely impressed not only with the participants but also with their enthusiasm to build permanent and lasting links between the two countries. The twenty who attended came from diverse backgrounds and worked in sectors such as law and justice, agriculture, health, education, the military, finance and tourism.

One of their very sensible recommendations is that an online teaching resource be developed for primary and high school students in both Australia and PNG to assist in understanding the nations' joint history. Another is that an expanded sister-city relationship could include town planning advice from Australian councils to help address some of the increasing strains facing PNG's fast-developing cities. One further recommendation that would really help promote a deeper understanding of PNG is the development of a professional exchange program that would enable Australians to take up work placements in Papua New Guinea while Papua New Guineans could gain valuable experience and know-how from taking up work placements in Australia. The idea is that the program would be aimed at mid-career applicants and be for placements of up to twelve months.[115]

Under the New Colombo Plan, a signature policy of Julie Bishop's that aims to improve the knowledge of the Indo-Pacific in Australia by supporting undergraduates to study in the region, Australian students are studying at the University of Goroka. One of the problems that PNG's tertiary institutions face is their inability to offer the sort of pay packages that would attract internationally recognised academic staff. One of the big mistakes that I believe we made in the early to mid 1970s when Australia and PNG were jointly implementing a rapid localisation policy (the replacement of Australians by generally much younger and inexperienced Papua New Guineans) was applying that policy to PNG's universities. For example, the University of Papua New Guinea had attracted some wonderful Australian academics in its early years and the quality of the graduates reflected that. The golden handshakes offered under the localisation policy meant many resumed their careers in Australia. So an enhanced program providing Australian academics with the salary top-ups necessary to encourage them to teach in PNG's tertiary institutions would certainly be worth the investment.

MEDIA

With the Australian media presence in PNG already dramatically reduced, it will be hard to convince the main commercial Australian media organisations to send a permanent correspondent to Port Moresby these days. Still, there are things that PNG could do to help attract greater coverage of PNG by the Australian media. The poor image that Papua New Guinea has in the Australian media is partly of its own making. It is a painful exercise if you are an Australian journalist wanting to visit PNG. Ben Packham, a journalist married to an Australian diplomat currently based in Port Moresby, wrote about this in a post on *The Interpreter*, the Lowy Institute's digital magazine. 'The PNG leadership is extremely sensitive about how the country is presented to the outside world,' he said, 'and – since most journalists who come here want to report on issues like crime, disease, sorcery and the treatment of women – it makes it hard for reporters to enter the country in the first place. All visa applications by journalists must be approved by the Prime Minister's office before they are dealt with by the country's immigration officials. Delays of many months are commonplace.'[116]

Even journalists who have shown a serious commitment to the country find it hugely frustrating. Rowan Callick, who received an OBE from the PNG

Government for services to journalism, applied with a photographer to cover the national elections in 2012. 'We finally got a positive response after about ten weeks,' he told Packham, 'some time after the campaign had finished!'[117]

CULTURE AND SPORT

Culture and sport are two areas where there is scope for improved connections between Australia and PNG. On the cultural front there are some bright spots these days, although few Australians know about them. David Bridie's Australian band, Not Drowning, Waving, which was around in the 1980s and early 1990s, visited PNG in 1988 and recorded their album *Tabaran* with one of PNG's top musicians, George Telek. After putting their album together in Melbourne, the band Not Drowning, Waving toured PNG and Australia and featured in an SBS documentary. The band broke up in 1994 but David Bridie continued working with George Telek, who recorded a solo album that won an ARIA award. He then helped Telek tour the world, performing in the United States, the United Kingdom, Europe and Australia. 'Telek showed a positive side to PNG,' Bridie says, 'so at odds with the normal assumptions of corruption, natural disasters and *raskol* gangs.' Bridie has gone on to form The Wantok Musik

Foundation as an Australian-based not-for-profit organisation which he says 'promotes and facilitates various cultural exchanges and a greater level of economic empowerment for Melanesian and indigenous artists and their communities'.

The Australian Museum in Sydney has what is undoubtedly the world's largest collection of ethnographic objects from Papua New Guinea. At its Pacific Spirit exhibition in late 2015 it displayed a limited number of what the museum described as 'rare and priceless artefacts' including '23 elaborate and sacred Malangan masks from Papua New Guinea dating from the 1800s'.[118] Some of these objects had real impact when the world became aware of them and they 'influenced the 20th century modernist movement and artists such as Matisse and Picasso'.[119]

Still, more than 31 000 other ethnographic items from PNG in the museum's collection have hardly ever been seen except by those who keep them stored in the museum's vaults. Other museums around Australia have PNG collections too, some of which are occasionally put on display. But, a bit like the relationship, much of it has been locked away in the basement, out of sight. It's time we put this marvellous collection on more regular and prominent display, and help new generations of Australians understand the great cultural depth and diversity of our nearest neighbour.

But if there is one area where people-to-people relations could achieve real depth, it is sport. PNG is the only country in the world where Rugby League is the major national sport. The PNG national team, the Kumuls, has played against the Australian Prime Minister's XIII every year since 2005. The game is staged in PNG late in the year when the NRL finals are drawing to a close in Australia and the Australian team is selected from players in teams already eliminated. One of the great challenges in PNG is creating a sense of national unity. Rugby League does it. On the Gold Coast in 2015, during Rugby League's international fixtures weekend, Papua New Guinea played Fiji while Samoa played Tonga. When the Kumuls went down to the Fiji Bati 22–10, angst burst out all over social media sites in PNG. 'We used to be Number Four in the World,' one contributor said demanding to know why the team had not won despite having Mal Meninga as the Kumul coach.

Only two PNG players who played in that tournament had contracts with NRL teams, but quite a few of the Fijians did and the entire teams representing Samoa and Tonga were first grade NRL players. How has this come about? It is not that Papua New Guineans cannot play. James Segeyaro, who plays for the Penrith Panthers, was the Hooker of the Year in the NRL in 2014. In Rugby Union, the Wallabies halfback, Will Genia, is a Papua New Guinean whose father is a former PNG defence minister. Segeyaro has lived in Australia since the age of seven, when he moved to Cairns with his mother. Genia was a star footballer while boarding at Brisbane Boys' College and was signed up to play for Queensland a year after representing the Australian Schoolboys side.

The reason there are so many Fijians, Samoans and Tongans playing Rugby League and Rugby Union in Australia is thanks to New Zealand's migration program. Samoa was a New Zealand colony and 1100 Samoan citizens can migrate to New Zealand every year under what is called the 'Samoan Quota Scheme'. The Fijians and Tongans get in under the 'Pacific Access Category', which allows 650 migrants a year. Once a resident, they can apply to bring other family members to New Zealand under the 'Family Sponsored' category and any migrant accepted under these schemes receives permanent residency. Cook Islanders automatically qualify for New Zealand permanent residency. Once accepted by New Zealand these Pacific Islanders can then come to Australia. And they have in droves. Despite the fact that PNG was our colony, Australia has no special migration scheme favouring Papua New

Guineans. According to the last Australian Census in 2011, of the 166 272 Pacific Islanders in Australia, 65 per cent are from Polynesia and just 35 per cent from Melanesia. Indeed, there are more Cook Islanders in Australia than Papua New Guineans even though PNG has more than 430 times the population of the Cooks – but, of course, the Cook Islands was a New Zealand colony![120]

John Wilshere, a former Kumul captain, says that most Australian NRL clubs would think it is not worth the bother to bring in a player from PNG. 'Say they look to sign a player from Papua New Guinea and he comes down as a fringe first grader, maybe on $50 000. The club will weigh up the options – do we invest in a Papua New Guinean player for this much money or can we invest in two juniors, for the same amount, who have already had that exposure to the development programs in Australia or New Zealand? The PNG player has possibly never been overseas before so you have to find him accommodation. And then it becomes a whole player welfare issue where you need to ensure that the player is being well looked after.' This is something Australia could look at under a sports aid program. For a modest outlay it could do wonders for PNG's national pride and unity to help a few more Papua New Guineans get the sort of NRL experience that might help take the Kumuls back to being one of the top four national rugby league teams in the world.

VISAS

Papua New Guineans are also seriously under-represented in Australia's Seasonal Worker Programme. This program allows companies to recruit Pacific Islanders to work in Australia's horticulture, accommodation, aquaculture, cane and cotton industries. The Pacific Seasonal Worker Pilot Scheme was introduced in 2008 and ran until mid-2012. Although the modest cap on the pilot program was 2500 workers, the numbers who came in to take up short-term employment fell well short of that at 1534. Of those, 1250 were Tongans while only 82 came in from PNG. A permanent scheme is now in place allowing Pacific Islanders to work in Australia 'for a single approved Australian employer for a period of between 14 weeks and 6 months'.[121] The cap on numbers for 2015/16 is 4250. New Zealand has a similar seasonal labour scheme which is working much better and takes twice as many Pacific Islanders.

The number of Papua New Guineans getting seasonal work in Australia remains very low. 'We need to get serious about offering labour mobility opportunities to those parts of the Pacific that most need it,' according to Jonathan Pryke of the Lowy Institute. 'New Zealand has been doing this for its former colony, Samoa, and other Polynesian countries over the last half-century. We have a long way to go to catch up.'[122] The Australian Department of Employment says 'there are no country quotas in the programme' in our scheme, but perhaps there should be. A quota system would give Papua New Guineans many of those seasonal jobs in Australia, which would allow the average worker to remit between A$5000 and A$6000 to their families back home.

The difficulty of getting a visa to Australia really rankles with Papua New Guineans, especially when it appears to them that it is easier for Samoans, Tongans, Cook Islanders and Fijians to get one. Julie Bishop has made it marginally easier than it was. Papua New Guineans who have obtained visas now have special lanes they can line up in at the Brisbane airport. But obstacles still remain in actually getting the visa issued and this annoys Prime Minister Peter O'Neill. He told the 31st Australia–Papua New Guinea Business Forum in Lae in May 2015 that 'this is an issue on which our two countries have held numerous discussions, but we have seen limited progress. I remain hopeful that this issue will be resolved [soon] – easing up visa access for Australians and Papua New Guineans alike.'[123]

On 1 March 2015 PNG cancelled the previous arrangement whereby Australians could pick up a visa for PNG on arrival. Australians now have to obtain a visa in advance and that has hurt PNG's tiny tourism industry. However, O'Neill said PNG was simply applying the same rules as Australia. 'This ease of movement, for business travellers and tourists, is important for both countries,' he said, 'but this has to be undertaken with fairness. We hope that there can be resolution in Canberra that is based on mutual respect.' He then went on to reveal that Indonesia was giving PNG a much better deal.[124]

There seems to be concern that Papua New Guineans will flood into Australia if the current restrictions are eased. The experience in the Torres Strait provides an indication of how unlikely that is. About 30 000 Papua New Guineans and 3000 Australians are able to travel across the border either way for traditional purposes – which also includes shopping trips – within a Protected Zone established under the Torres Strait Treaty. Around 50 000 crossings are made each year and rather than pose a threat to Australia, the PNG villagers regularly report on any illegal movement they see. 'We know which people are from those Australian islands and they know who we are,' Robinson Gibuna, a pastor at PNG's Sigabaduru Village told me. 'And any strange person trying to go across, trying to use our identity, will be caught easily.'[125] The Papua New Guineans in those villages are actually helping protect our borders!

Forty years on

While I believe that too many Australians know too little about PNG, there are those who are absolutely committed to the country. There are truly dedicated Australians working for the major Christian churches and doing remarkable work in health and education. It would be wonderful if their stories could reach a bigger audience. Similarly, Australian Volunteers International has placed people in PNG positions since the mid-1960s. A number of Australian NGOs are heavily involved. One NGO established to recognise our World War II debt to Papua New Guineans is the Kokoda Track Foundation. This was partly inspired by the several thousand trekkers who cross the 90-kilometre jungle track each year. 'We've been working across the Kokoda catchment region for the past decade and we work with about forty-five elementary and primary schools,' says Genevieve Nelson, CEO and one of the founding directors. 'We do a range of things to support the operations of those schools, starting with teacher training but also supporting their salaries if and when the government system is not working.' A survey the foundation conducted six weeks into the 2015 school year found problems with delivery in the O'Neill government's free schooling program. 'In about 80 per cent of cases the tuition-free subsidies had not yet been received,' Nelson says.[126]

The foundation has built a teacher training college at Kokoda. 'The actual capital costs of the infrastructure have been around the A$700 000 mark,' Nelson told me. 'That's been thanks to an enormous philanthropic contribution from supplies of materials, to volunteers going up to build the college – materials have gone up from Australia through low-bono shipping services from shipping companies. It has been a couple of years of a lot of hard work and we have finally got the School of Education campus up, and now we're working on the School of Health which means that alongside training teachers we'll be training health workers.'

Each year, sixty elementary teachers and sixty health workers will be enrolled at the college. Nelson says the biggest focus of the School of Education is training quality teachers. 'We're running a forty-week elementary teacher training program as opposed to the government-run six-week program. It is still very much based on the PNG curriculum and syllabus but it's stretched out across those forty weeks with a lot of additional components added. So there's a strong focus on pedagogy, on child behaviour, on nutrition, sport and how to be the most innovative teacher you can be. After your training, you are most likely to be posted to a remote rural area, you may never get a mentor, you may never get given special development, you may or may not get government support. So what do we need to do with them in this year of training to set them on that path to be the best teacher they can be.'[127]

The head of the School of Education is a Papua New Guinean, Petra Arifeae. 'She is a star,' says Nelson. 'She has twenty years' teaching experience in PNG and she was working with us down in Sydney for a couple of years, helping us develop this new teacher training program. Petra has piloted this over the past two-and-a-half years with a cohort that we have been taking through.'[128]

One ex-soldier with a close PNG connection is Australia's former Governor-General, Major General Michael Jeffery. From 1974 to 1975 he was the Commanding Officer of the Second Battalion of

PNG's Pacific Islands Regiment based in Wewak. These days he is the patron of the Papua New Guinea Association of Australia (PNGAA), which devotes itself to promoting what it calls the 'special relationship' between Australia and its former colony. The PNGAA was originally set up as the Retired Officers' Association of PNG in 1951 to safeguard the interests and retirement conditions of superannuated Australian public servants who had worked there. Over the years its role has expanded to include supporting projects in PNG and holding an annual conference promoting the relationship. It now has 1500 members, publishes a quarterly journal *Una Voce* and preserves a significant quantity of historical materials related to PNG.

When Papua New Guineans reflect on the past forty years of PNG's independence from Australia, many do it with mixed emotions. 'On September the 16th 1975, I was one of those who waved the flag at Sir Hubert Murray Stadium as a Sogeri Senior High School student,' says John Eggins, former news editor at EMTV. 'We were amongst the main celebrants on independence day, and I waved the flag wondering what would happen. And, to tell you the truth, I am still wondering today. Papua New Guinea has come this far. I think we could have gone a lot further than we have. A lot of things have gone wrong.

Some have gone right but the wrong has simply outweighed the right in our path to progress I suppose. It is true that PNG is one of the most complex countries in the world. That should have been the cue in the beginning to say, "Hang on! Are we going to unite all those tribes? Are we going to get people together because of the way we are located, the geography of the country is difficult" and things like that. That should have been a yellow flag, if you will, to say, "Hang on! Are we ready for independence?" To me, independence was an emotional thing. It was an emotional decision more than it was backed by economics, social development and whatever else that makes a nation a nation. The tribes, the different regions, the Highlands, the Coastals, the Islands! The suspicion that existed at that time amongst the various groups and the various peoples – that suspicion still exists today. It exists in the administration, in politics, in business, in whatever else. The Highlanders are still suspicious of the Sepiks and vice versa. It is all there still.'[129]

Eggins suspects Australia was more than happy to be rid of its colony. 'Was Australia getting rid of a thorn in its rib at that time?' he asks. 'And, today, if you look at the way Australia deals with its Indigenous population, the Aborigines, the track record is not an impressive one. And the Australian political leadership admits that.' He says he can understand why Australians have such difficulty coming to terms with Papua New Guinea, a country filled to the brim with indigenous people speaking 860 different languages. 'We are too complex. We are too aggressive in a lot of ways and we don't operate the Westminster system in the way that they are used to. So they find us irrational.'[130] Papua New Guineans are not irrational. The more you get to know them and understand them the more admiration you have for the way they are trying to forge a way through the confusion resulting from having been thrust into making a nation out of a thousand tribes.

When I asked PNG Prime Minister Peter O'Neill why Australians should take a greater interest in his country he said he would like Australians to realise how important the relationship is. 'We are your closest neighbour,' O'Neill said. 'We have got an economy that is growing very fast which is providing many opportunities for Australians. The distance is not too far. It is only an hour from Cairns. And we have a very robust democracy that is continuing to mature. We also have to take note of the fact that a lot of young people of both countries died in the conflicts of World War II. More Australians died in Papua New Guinea in that war than anywhere else in the world. I know that Australians have a focus elsewhere. But the more that we can educate the young population in Australia about some of these issues and the historical relationship and the significance of that the better it will be.'[131]

Sir Julius Chan is concerned that the relationship that carried over from the colonial era and the war years has almost disappeared because the human element is fading away. 'I think that the Australia–PNG relationship is losing touch very fast,' he told me. 'And if we treat the relationship as a money issue and an aid issue there won't be any longer any human face in it. And I think the lustre of our relationship will have been lost.' The Secretary of the Department of Foreign Affairs and Trade, Peter Varghese, told the Lowy Institute that PNG's 'stability matters to Australia' and that the Australian market has a large role to play in PNG's prosperity. 'In the past our relationship has been dominated by aid,' he said. 'The future however will need to focus more on partnership. Perhaps more than any other single relationship, the state of our relationship with PNG is seen as a barometer of Australian foreign policy success.'[132]

Australians need to work on our side of the relationship. I find it difficult to understand why Papua New Guinea and Australia's role in its creation as an independent country is not part of school curricula throughout Australia. While there were some things from the colonial era that we should not celebrate, helping give birth to another nation should have been one of our proudest achievements. Instead, we seem to have become so embarrassed by our performance and so politically correct that we don't want to teach our children that we were colonialists ourselves once. Throwing money at PNG is definitely not enough. If we are to have a relationship that is a 'barometer' of Australia's success in foreign policy then we need to understand PNG. And that is not easy. As Sir Kostas Constantino puts it: 'People who come to PNG with management degrees find it perplexing – you might as well take the degree and throw it in the rubbish bin. Start learning again! It is hard yakka.'[133]

We need to start learning more about Papua New Guinea and treating it as an equal – not as our unfortunate illegitimate child that we are ashamed of. Papua New Guinea is a country worth having as a good, solid, friendly neighbour. It is time to stop being the embarrassed colonialist, embrace our history in PNG, both good and bad, and build a new partnership with one of our most vibrant neighbours.

Endnotes

1   Interview with the author, 6 March 2015.

2   Interview with the author, 11 March 2015.

3   Alex Oliver, 'Lowy Institute Poll 2015', Lowy Institute for International Policy, p.17.

4   Tim Bowden, *Taim Bilong Masta: Australian Involvement in Papua New Guinea*, ABC Radio Series, Program 1 'Never a Colony' (1982).

5   Ibid.

6   Ibid.

7   Sean Dorney, *Papua New Guinea: People, Politics and History since 1975* (Sydney: ABC Books, 2000), pp. 27–28.

8   *Taim Bilong Masta*, Program 21 'Courts and Calaboose' (1982).

9   Dorney, *Papua New Guinea: People, Politics and History since 1975*, pp. 28–29.

10 Dorney family files.

11 Paul Hasluck, *A Time for Building: Australian Administration in Papua and New Guinea, 1951–1963* (Carlton, Vic.: Melbourne University Press, 1976).

12 Ibid.

13 Ibid.

14 Interview with the author, 12 March 2015.

15 Ibid.

16 Tim Bowden's epic eighteen hour–long *Taim Bilong Masta* radio series bears testimony to the passion and commitment of many of those who served in PNG during the colonial era.

17 Personal communication, July 2015.

18 Ibid.

19 Foreign Minister Julie Bishop, Remarks at Australia–PNG Emerging Leaders Dialogue, Lowy Institute for International Policy, 26 November 2013, soundcloud.com/lowyinstitute/australia-png-emerging-leaders-dialogue-2013.

20 Ibid.

21 Interview with the author, 17 April 2015.

22 *Taim Bilong Masta*, Program 4 'The Loneliness and the Glory' (1982).

23 Sean Dorney (reporter), 'Papua New Guinea', ABC *Foreign Correspondent*, 24 June 1997.

24 Ibid.

25 The Hon. Peter O'Neill, Address to Australia–PNG
Business Council, 17 March 2015.

26 The strongest critics of MPs' DSIP and other expenditures
is to be found in well-informed critiques on PNG's libellous
and sometimes scandal-mongering blogs, such as PNG
Blog, Sharp Talk and PNG News.

27 Interview with the author, 6 March 2015.

28 Interview with the author, 6 March 2015.

29 Interview with the author, 14 May 2015.

30 Auditor-General's Office of Paua New Guinea, 'District
Services Improvement Program – Report 3', 18 February
2014, p. 5, pngexposed.files.wordpress.com/2014/10/
report_no3_dsip.pdf.

31 The Ombudsman Commission in PNG has the job of
enforcing a broad Leadership Code set down in the
Constitution. It reads: 'A leader has a duty to conduct
himself in such a way, both in his public or official life and
his private life, and in his associations with other persons,
as not: (a) to place himself in a position to which he has or
could have a conflict of interest or might be compromised
when discharging his duties; or (b) to demean his office or
position; or (c) to allow his public or official integrity to be
called into question; or (d) to endanger or diminish respect
for and confidence in the integrity of government in Papua
New Guinea. In particular a leader shall not, (e) use his
office for personal gain, or (f) enter into any transaction or
engage in any enterprise or activity that might be expected
to give rise to doubt in the public mind as to whether he
is carrying out or had carried out the duty imposed by
the above.' Leadership Tribunals headed by a judge hear
Leadership Code cases and a score of politicians have been

dismissed from parliament since 1975 after being found
guilty of misconduct in office.

32 Interview with the author, 20 March 2015.

33 Hank Nelson, *Taim Bilong Masta: The Australian
    Involvement with Papua New Guinea* (Crows Nest,
    NSW: ABC Enterprises for the Australian Broadcasting
    Corporation, 1982), p. 18.

34 Hasluck, *A Time for Building*.

35 ACT NOW! function and interview with the author,
    5 March 2015.

36 Ibid.

37 Interview with the author, 9 March 2015.

38 Interview with the ABC's Trevor Watson quoted in Dorney,
    *Papua New Guinea: People, Politics and History since
    1975*, p. 294.

39 Quoted in Sean Dorney, *The Sandline Affair: Politics and
    Mercenaries and the Bougainville Crisis* (Sydney: ABC
    Books, 1998), p. 17.

40 Dorney, *Papua New Guinea: People, Politics and History
    since 1975*, pp.304–305

41 David Connery and Karl Claxton, 'Shared Interests,
    Enduring Cooperation: The Future of Australia–PNG
    Police Engagement', Australian Strategic Policy Institute,
    Special Report, October 2014.

42 Ibid, p. 26.

43 Sadaf Lakhani and Alys M Willman, *Trends in Crime
    and Violence in Papua New Guinea* (Washington DC:

The World Bank, 2014).

44 Connery and Claxton, 'Shared Interests, Enduring
    Cooperation: The Future of Australia–PNG Police
    Engagement'.

45 Human Rights Watch, 'World Report 2015: Papua New
    Guinea – Country Summary', January 2015,
    p. 2, www.hrw.org/sites/default/files/related_material/
    papuanewguinea.pdf.

46 Ibid.

47 Interview with the author, 8 March 2015.

48 Interview with the author, 9 March 2015.

49 Asian Development Bank, *Asian Development Outlook
    2015: Financing Asia's Future Growth*, March 2015,
    www.adb.org/sites/default/files/publication/154508/
    ado-2015.pdf.

50 Bank of Papua New Guinea, *Monetary Policy Statement*,
    31 March 2015, www.bankpng.gov.pg/wp-content/
    uploads/2015/03/2015-March-MPS.pdf.

51 The Hon Peter O'Neill, Address to the Lowy Institute for
    International Policy, 14 May 2015, www.lowyinstitute.
    org/publications/address-hon-peter-oneill-cmg-mp-prime-
    minister-papua-new-guinea.

52 Rebecca Hyam, 'Woodside Surprised, Disappointed After
    Oil Search Takeover Bid Rejected', ABC news report, 16
    October 2015, www.abc.net.au/news/2015-09-14/oil-
    search-rejects-woodside-takeover-bid/6773962.

53 Oil Search, Submission to Joint Standing Committee on
    Foreign Affairs, Defence and Trade, 'Inquiry into the Role
    of the Private Sector in Promoting Economic Growth and

Reducing Poverty in the Indo-Pacific Region', 8 May 2014.

54 Interview with the author, 11 March 2015.

55 Paul Flanagan, 'PNG's Frightening Fiscal Figures', DevPolicy, 5 August 2015, devpolicy.org/pngs-frightening-fiscal-figures-20150805/.

56 John Garnaut, 'Papua New Guinea Hurt by Commodities Drop, on Brink of Greek-style Crisis', *Sydney Morning Herald*, 6 August 2015, www.smh.com.au/world/papua-new-guinea-hurt-by-commodities-drop-on-brink-of-greekstyle-crisis-20150805-gisodr.html.

57 Dorney, *The Sandline Affair*.

58 Interview with the author, 13 March 2015.

59 Sean Dorney, *Paradise Imperfect*, Episode 2, ABC Television (2000).

60 Interview with the author, 13 March 2015.

61 Ibid.

62 Ibid.

63 Interview with the author, 11 March 2015.

64 Interview with the author, 9 March 2015.

65 Item on *The World*, ABC 24 and Australia Network, 30 July 2014.

66 Interview with the author, 6 March 2015.

67 Interview with the author, 7 March 2015.

68 Carnival Australia, 'Princess Cruises Offers a Memorable Voyage for Anzac Veteran', 28 April 2015, www.carnivalaustralia.com/media-releases/2015/april/princess-cruises-offers-a-memorable-voyage-for-anzac-veteran.aspx.

69 Interview with the author, 5 March 2015.

70 Ibid.

71 Interview with the author, 10 March 2015.

72 Interview with the author, 5 March 2015.

73 Interview with the author, 9 March 2015.

74 Ibid.

75 Ibid.

76 Interview with the author, 11 March 2015.

77 Department of Foreign Affairs Budget Portfolio 2015/16, dfat.gov.au/about-us/corporate/portfolio-budget-statements/Pages/budget-highlights-2015-16.aspx.

78 O'Neill, Address to the Lowy Institute for International Policy, 14 May 2015.

79 Liam Cochrane, 'Papua New Guinea Bans Australians from Travelling to Bougainville', ABC news report, 18 May 2015, www.abc.net.au/news/2015-05-18/png-government-bans-australians-from-travelling-to-bougainville/6478378.

80 Interview with the author, 7 March 2015.

81 Edward Wolfers quoted in Dorney, *The Sandline Affair*, pp. 338–339.

82 Interview with the author, 18 March 2015.

83 Interview with the author, 20 March 2015.

84 Liam Cochrane, 'Australia Withdraws Funding from Papua New Guinea Health Programs Over Corruption, Fake Drug Concerns', ABC news report, 26 December 2013, www.abc.net.au/news/2013-12-26/an-australia-cuts-funding-of-png-medical-kits/5174992.

85 Interview with the author, 6 March 2015.

86 Ibid.

87 *Taim Bilong Masta*, Program 2 'The Good Time Before' (1982).

88 Commonwealth of Australia, *Defence White Paper 2013* (Canberra: Department of Defence, 2013), www.defence.gov.au/whitepaper/2013/docs/WP_2013_web.pdf.

89 Jenny Hayward-Jones, 'Australia's Costly Investment in Solomon Islands: The Lessons of RAMSI', Lowy Institute Analysis, 8 May 2014, www.lowyinstitute.org/publications/lessons-ramsi.

90 Interview with the author, 6 March 2015.

91 Jonathan Schultz, 'Novel for its Lack of Novelty: Gillard in Papua New Guinea', *The Conversation*, theconversation.com/novel-for-its-lack-of-novelty-gillard-in-papua-new-guinea-14071.

92 'Asylum Seekers Arriving in Australia by Boat to be Resettled in Papua New Guinea', ABC news report, 20 July 2013, www.abc.net.au/news/2013-07-19/manus-island-detention-centre-to-be-expanded-under-rudd27s-asy/4830778.

93 Communication with various people from Manus
    Province.

94 Bob Carr, *Diary of a Foreign Minister* (Sydney: NewSouth
    Publishing, 2014).

95 Daniel Flitton, 'Carr Threatens to Hit PNG with
    Sanctions', *Sydney Morning Herald*, 15 March 2012,
    www.smh.com.au/federal-politics/political-news/carr-
    threatens-to-hit-png-with-sanctions-20120314-1v3zs.html.

96 Dorney, *The Sandline Affair*, pp. 343–344.

97 Interview with the author, 5 March 2015.

98 Interview with the author, 9 March 2015.

99 Interview with the author, 10 March 2015.

100 Jo Chandler, 'Violence Against Women in PNG: How Men
    Are Getting Away with Murder', Lowy Institute Analysis,
    29 August 2014, www.lowyinstitute.org/publications/
    violence-against-women-png-how-men-are-getting-away-
    murder.

101 *The National* quoted in Dorney, *The Sandline Affair*.

102 Samantha Maiden, 'How Some Cannibals, a Throne
    and a Hairy Pig Won Over Foreign Minister Bob Carr',
    Sunday Herald Sun, 9 December 2012, www.theaustralian.
    com.au/news/how-some-cannibals-a-throne-and-a-
    hairy-pig-won-over-foreign-minister-bob-carr/story-
    e6frg6n6-1226532745297.

103 Interview with the author, 7 March 2015.

104 Interview with the author, 17 April 2015.

105 Alex Oliver, 'The Lowy Institute Poll 2015', Lowy Institute for International Policy (2015), p. 15.

106 Joint Committee on Foreign Affairs, Defence and Trade, *Australia's Relations with Papua New Guinea* (Canberra: Parliament of the Commonwealth, 1991).

107 Ibid.

108 Interview with the author, 23 March 2013.

109 'PNG PM to Crackdown on Aid Middlemen', *Courier-Mail*, 3 August 2015, www.couriermail.com.au/news/breaking-news/png-pm-to-crackdown-on-aid-middlemen/story-fnihsfrf-1227467601101.

110 Prime Minister's Office of Papua New Guinea, 'Papua New Guinea Plans Rethink of Development Support Delivery – Enough of Aid Industry Middlemen', news release, 3 August 2015, www.officeofprimeminister.com/#!-Papua-New-Guinea-Plans-Rethink-of-Development-Support-Delivery–Enough-of-Aid-Industry-Middlemen-/c248k/55beb0970cf267673a81064f.

111 Ibid. In 2014 private contractors received A$281 million from the PNG aid budget: Department of Foreign Affairs and Trade submission to Parliamentary Inquiry on 'The Delivery and Effectiveness of Australia's Bilateral Aid Program in Papua New Guinea', April 2015.

112 Ibid.

113 Ibid.

114 Minister for Foreign Affairs, Julie Bishop, 'Papua New Guinea: Pacific Leadership and Governance Precinct Launch', media release, 6 November 2015, foreignminister.gov.au/releases/Pages/2015/jb_mr_151106a.aspx.

115 Jenny Hayward-Jones, Mark Tamsitt and Anna Kirk, '2014 Australia–Papua New Guinea Emerging Leaders Dialogue: Outcomes Report', 20 January 2015, lowyinstitute.org/publications/2014-australia-papua-new-guinea-emerging-leaders-dialogue-outcomes-report.

116 Ben Packham, 'Telling Tales Part 2 – The Current State of Australian Reporting on PNG (and why is it the way it is?)', Australia–Papua New Guinea Network, Lowy Institute for International Policy, 13 November 2014, auspng.lowyinstitute.org/publications/telling-tales-part-2-current-state-australian-reporting-png-and-why-it-way-it.

117 Ibid.

118 *Pacific Spirit*, Australian Museum exhibition, australianmuseum.net.au/event/pacific-spirit#sthash.GdPRqwsI.dpuf.

119 'Masks from Melanesia', Australian Museum, australianmuseum.net.au/masks-from-melanesia.

120 Jonathan Pryke, 'Pacific Islanders in Australia: Where Are the Melanesians?', *DevPolicy Blog*, 28 August 2014, devpolicy.org/pacific-islanders-in-australia-where-are-the-melanesians-20140828/.

121 Department of Employment, 'Seasonal Worker Programme', employment.gov.au/seasonal-worker-programme.

122 Pryke, 'Pacific Islanders in Australia: Where Are the Melanesians?'.

123 The Hon Peter O'Neill, Address to the Papua New Guinea–Australia Business Forum, Lae, 18 May 2015, www.pm.gov.pg/images/SP-PM_PNG-AU_Business_Forum-150518F_1.pdf.

124 Ibid.

125 Sean Dorney, 'Border Patrol: Torres Strait Edition',
    Correspondents Report, ABC Radio National,
    17 November 2013, www.abc.net.au/correspondents/
    content/2013/s3892469.htm.
126 Interview with the author, 24 April 2015.

127 Ibid.

128 Ibid.

129 Interview with the author, 10 March 2015.

130 Ibid.

131 Interview with the author, 14 May 2015.

132 Peter Varghese, 'An Australian World View:
    A Practitioner's Perspective', Address at the Lowy
    Institute for International Policy, 20 August 2015, www.
    lowyinstitute.org/publications/australian-world-view-
    practitioners-perspective.

133 Interview with the author, 11 March 2015.

Acknowledgements

The Lowy Institute's Melanesia Program Director, Jenny Hayward-Jones, suggested I tackle the Australia–PNG relationship forty years on from PNG's independence. Anthony Bubalo, the Lowy Institute's Research Director, took on the unenviable task of reigning in my enthusiasm on the subject and keeping this Lowy Paper within the desired length. I would like to thank the reviewers, Bill Standish, Ted Wolfers and Ian Kemish, for their helpful comments, queries and corrections – in particular Ian Kemish, a former Australian High Commissioner to PNG who was happy to take a call and enlighten me on one or two matters. The reviewers did not all agree with everything that is in the final product and the responsibility for any failings still in the Paper are entirely mine. Lowy Institute Research

Associate, Philippa Brant, and Research Editor, Lydia Papandrea, tidied up the later drafts, and Cate Blake at Penguin brought it all together. My deepest thanks go to the many people in Papua New Guinea who so generously agreed to be interviewed for this Paper and those who provided me with background information.

Lowy Institute Papers

1. *India: The next economic giant*, Mark Thirlwell (2004)

2. *River at risk: The Mekong and the water politics of China and Southeast Asia*, Milton Osborne (2004)

3. *Unsheathing the Samurai sword: Japan's changing security policy*, Alan Dupont (2004)

4. *Diaspora: The world wide web of Australians*, Michael Fullilove and Chloe Flutter (2004)

5. *Joining the caravan? The Middle East, Islamism and Indonesia*, Anthony Bubalo and Greg Fealy (2005)

6. *Balancing act: Taiwan's cross-strait challenge*, Malcolm Cook and Craig Meer (2005)

7. *The new terms of trade*, Mark Thirlwell (2005)

8. *Permanent friends? Historical reflections on the Australian-American alliance*, Peter Edwards (2005)

9. *Re-imagining PNG: Culture, democracy and Australia's role*, Ben Scott (2005)

10. *Shared secrets: Intelligence and collective security*, Simon Chesterman (2006)

11. *The paramount power: China and the countries of Southeast Asia*, Milton Osborne (2006)

12. *Heating up the planet: Climate change and security*, Alan Dupont and Graeme Pearman (2006)

13. *Pitfalls of Papua: Understanding the conflict and its place in Australia-Indonesia relations*, Rodd McGibbon (2006)

14. *Quiet boom: How the long economic upswing is changing Australia and its place in the world*, John Edwards (2006)

15. *Howard's decade: An Australian foreign policy reappraisal*, Paul Kelly (2006)

16. *Beyond the defence of Australia: Finding a new balance in Australian strategic policy*, Hugh White (2006)

17. *Mindanao: A gamble worth taking*, Malcolm Cook and Kit Collier (2006)

18. *Second thoughts on globalisation*, Mark Thirlwell (2007)

19. *Australia and Indonesia: Current problems, future prospects*, Jamie Mackie (2007)

20. *Enmeshed: Australia and Southeast Asia's fisheries*, Meryl Williams (2007)

21. *The end of the Vasco da Gama era: The next landscape of world politics*, Coral Bell (2007)

22. *World wide webs: Diasporas and the international system*, Michael Fullilove (2008)

23. *The emerging global order: Australian foreign policy in the 21st century*, Russell Trood (2008)

24. *Into Africa: How the resource boom is making sub-Saharan Africa more important to Australia*, Roger Donnelly and Benjamin Ford (2008)

25. *Zealous democrats: Islamism and democracy in Egypt, Indonesia and Turkey*, Anthony Bubalo, Greg Fealy and Whit Mason (2008)

26. *A focused force: Australia's defence priorities in the Asian century*, Hugh White (2009)

27. *Confronting the hydra: Big problems with small wars*, Mark O'Neill (2009)

28. *China and the global environment: Learning from the past, anticipating the future*, Katherine Morton (2009)

29. *The Mekong: River under threat*, Milton Osborne (2009)

30. *Confronting ghosts: Thailand's shapeless southern insurgency*, Don Pathan and Joseph Chinyong Liow (2010)

31. *Courting reform: Indonesia's Islamic courts and justice for the poor*, Cate Sumner and Tim Lindsey (2010)

LOWY INSTITUTE PENGUIN SPECIALS

32. *Beyond the Boom*, John Edwards (2014)

33. *The Adolescent Country*, Peter Hartcher (2014)

34. *Condemned to Crisis?*, Ken Ward (2015)

OTHER PENGUIN SPECIALS
YOU COULD TRY:

Beauty's Sister	James Bradley
Rudd, Gillard and Beyond	Troy Bramston
Governor Bligh and the Short Man	Peter Cochrane
Utzon and the Sydney Opera House	Daryl Dellora
The Coal Face	Tom Doig
The Absent Therapist	Will Eaves
Beyond the Boom	John Edwards
The Ellis Laws	Bob Ellis
The Badlands	Paul French
The Girl with the Dogs	Anna Funder
The Rise and Fall of the House of Bo	John Garnaut
The Deserted Newsroom	Gideon Haigh
End of the Road?	Gideon Haigh
The Adolescent Country	Peter Hartcher
Life in Ten Houses	Sonya Hartnett
The Simple Life	Rhonda Hetzel
Does Cooking Matter?	Rebecca Huntley
Take Your Best Shot	Jacqueline Kent
What Would Gandhi Do?	Michael Kirby

OTHER PENGUIN SPECIALS
YOU COULD TRY: CONTINUED

A Story of Grief	Michaela McGuire
The Tunnel	Dennis McIntosh
Mistakes Were Made	Liam Pieper
Ballots, Bullets and Kabulshit	Toby Ralph
Is There No Place for Me?	Kate Richards
Salad Days	Ronnie Scott
The First Dismissal	Luke Slattery
Reclaiming Epicurus	Luke Slattery
After Cancer	Dr Ranjana Srivastava
Dying for a Chat	Dr Ranjana Srivastava
You're Just Too Good To Be True	Sofija Stefanovic
Condemned to Crisis?	Ken Ward